NINEWELLS REVISITED

DR TOM SOMMERVILLE AND ALAN WIGHTMAN

Published by Balallan House, Inveralavaig, Portree, Isle of Skye, Scotland, IV51 9NG
Email: alanwightman@isleofskye.me.uk

ISBN number : 978-0-956 1438-0-8

This book is dedicated to the memory of Dr Tom Sommerville who believed in the necessity of an objective study of this new model of a teaching hospital, to the concept and planning of which he made a major contribution.

As we go to print, the death of Sir Lewis Robertson on the 24th November 2008 was intimated. Sir Lewis will be remembered for his contributions to Scottish life and to his native city of Dundee. In an important sense, 'Ninewells Revisited' is a tribute to his leadership throughout the duration of the project. Without his help and encouragement in writing the story of Ninewells, it might have remained in dusty half-forgotten files.

FOREWORD

Ninewells Hospital and Medical School was intended to be a new model of a modern teaching hospital. The University Grants Committee had set the scene in its decision that it was to be a unified entity on a single site. This was the bedrock from which the Brief and the Design were to be constructed.

A strategic approach by the Hospital Board and St Andrews University resulted in the setting up of a Joint Planning Committee composed of representatives of the Board, the University, and the Scottish Health Department. The principal aim of the Committee was to achieve an orderly process of consultations where new thinking was to be found and new solutions to specific problems to be explored. In this regard the work of the Nuffield Trust played an important role.

Good teamwork ensured good progress leading to construction of full-scale mock-ups of selected parts of the hospital and medical school; the Scottish Office had set aside a substantial sum for this purpose. The many people who visited the mock-up programmes expressed strong support for the use of full-scale mock-ups as the means by which new ideas could be properly understood and tested against conventional wisdom.

The extensive work in establishing the Brief and the Design proposals was marred by a decision of the Department to extend the life of the Dundee Royal Infirmary. This was to enable certain major surgical facilities to be located in this old hospital. The decision of the University Grants Committee which envisaged Ninewells Teaching Hospital to be on a single site was thus overturned, with predictable consequences.

The verdict of medical staff and patients has been to welcome a truly modern teaching hospital, a verdict that has been echoed by the many visitors from home and abroad.

Sir Lewis Robertson
Chairman of the Joint Planning Committee

DESIGN TEAM

Architect	Robert Matthew, Johnson-Marshall & Partners London, Edinburgh and Dundee
Structural Engineer	Ove Arup & Partners London, Edinburgh and Dundee
Services Engineer	Steensen, Varming and Mulcahy Copenhagen, Dublin and Dundee
Quantity Surveyor	W J R Christie & Partners Dundee

CONTENTS

PREFACE

The start of the Ninewells story could be said to have occurred in July 1960 with a special edition of The Architects' Journal on hospital design. Eight of the contributers to this edition came from the 'Ninewells Team'.

When the decision in 1949 was made to build a new teaching hospital in Dundee, the Eastern Regional Hospital Board and St Andrews University were faced with a considerable challenge. No new teaching hospital had been built in the UK since the latter half of the nineteenth Century; hence there was a substantial lack of knowledge.

The purpose of this Study is threefold:- Firstly, it is to explain how the Hospital Board and the University responded to the challenge of designing a modern teaching hospital as proposed by the University Grants Committee. Secondly, it is to explain how the operational policies adopted in the Brief were interpreted. Thirdly, it is to draw some conclusions and to provide a critique relating to the experience in achieving what is widely regarded as an outstanding hospital and medical school in the City of Discovery.

Fig 1 RRS Discovery

At the outset it was intended that for the Study to be of value, it had to be objective, balanced and a readable story. It was no easy assignment.

For a vision of such a complex project, new ways of thinking and analysis were needed in order to bring new knowledge to the table.

It was not all plain sailing. Certain matters which refer to the building stage and the administration of the project caused difficulties; they have only been touched upon.

"The process of planning is like a complicated and never finished game of chess. In both you have to study existing situations carefully before making any move and then try and turn difficulties into opportunities" Sir Patrick Geddes

ACKNOWLEDGMENTS

The proposal for an objective study of the briefing, design, building and experience in use of Ninewells Hospital and Medical School came from Dr Tom Sommerville Senior Lecturer in the Department of Bacteriology, Queens College, Dundee. He was a pivotal player who acted as the bridge between the Hospital Board and the University in the compilation of the Brief, and throughout the Design Stages. His belief that the achievement of such an innovative project should not be lost to collective memory is the origin of this Study. It is to be seen as significant in the recent history of hospital and medical school design, and in the emergence of Dundee as a centre of excellence in medical research and the life sciences. The proposal for such a study was broadly welcomed by Tayside NHS Board and the Faculty of Medicine of the University of Dundee.

In the preparation of this Study, we would like to acknowledge the active help and encouragement received from the former Chairman of the Eastern Regional Hospital Board, Sir Lewis Robertson CBE. From his appointment in 1960, Sir Lewis was closely involved in the briefing, design, and building stages of Ninewells. Sir Malcolm Knox, former Principal of St Andrews University, acted jointly with Sir Lewis in steering the project to a successful completion.

Other key players were Professor Sir Robert Hunter (later Lord Hunter of Newington) former Dean of the Faculty of Medicine, Professor Sir Donald Douglas former Professor of Surgery, Dr James Hunter former Senior Administrative Medical Officer at the Hospital Board, and Mr James K Johnston OBE former Secretary to the Hospital Board who kept the ship on a steady course.

The untimely death of Dr Tom Sommerville interrupted progress at the midway stage of the Study, but with the encouragement of Sir Lewis Robertson work resumed with the help of Dr Graham Lowe Consultant Dermatologist and Honorary Curator of Tayside Medical History Museum.

We would also like to thank the following participants in the Study for their help in reviewing experience in use in the Hospital and the Medical School :
John Musgrove and Brigadier Welch of Nuffield Provincial Hospitals Trust, Professor Charles Forbes former Professor of Medicine, Mr Michael Lyall former Medical Director, Mr Murray Petrie Vice-Chair of Tayside NHS Board, Mr Robert Wood Consultant Surgeon, Professor Martin Pippard Dean of the Medical School, Dr Bill Morrison Head of the Accident and Emergency Service, Mr Robert Paton former Project Administrator at the Hospital Board, Professor Brian Burchell former Dean of the Faculty of Medicine, Dr Derek McLean former Medical Director, Professor Sir Philip Cohen Director of Research in the College of Life Sciences, Dr Gabrielle Phillips Consultant Medical Microbiologist, Sister Sheila Petrie, Sean Mulcahy of Steensen, Varming & Mulcahy, John MacBeath Building Manager, Alf Small and Peter Simpson of Ninewells Estates Department and W.J.R. Christie quantity surveyor.

We also wish to thank Stewart Clark, William Cadell and Ian Roy, senior architects in the Hawkhill House Team, along with librarian Gwyneth Smart and Jim Eaton.

The award from the Strathmartine Trust towards the cost of undertaking this work is gratefully acknowledged; without it the Study might not have got underway. We also wish to acknowledge the important financial contribution by NHS Tayside towards meeting the cost of publication of the book.

We also wish to record our thanks for the help and support received from the University of Dundee Archive Services, from the Dundee Heritage Trust, from David Winter & Son Ltd. of Dundee, from Duncan Macrae of 3D Komputers Portree, and from Gregor and Nancy Wightman for their help in bringing the work to fruition.

We acknowledge with thanks the photographs provided by A.L. Hunter, Henk Snoek, D.C.Thomson & Co, Keith Hunter, John Dewar Studios, Eric de Maré, Ron Gazzard, and the University of Dundee Archive Services. We also wish to thank the Dundee Heritage Trust for the photo of the RRS Discovery, berthed at Discovery Quay.

Fig 2 Aerial view of Menzieshill farm

INTRODUCTION

The seeds of Dundee's future reputation in the field of medicine and the life sciences were sown in the years prior to World War II by individuals such as Sir D'Arcy Thompson, Sir Patrick Geddes, Dr George Pirie and others keen to apply new knowledge in medicine and in public health. The legacy of Florence Nightingale is seen in the Victorian hospitals which remain in service in many of our larger towns and cities. In the immediate post-war years it was evident that modern medicine could not be taught and practiced satisfactorily in these hospitals. New solutions were necessary for the teaching of medicine, and for the battle against disease.

In 1949 the Eastern Regional Hospital Board and the University of St Andrews put forward proposals for a new hospital and a new medical school in Dundee. The site of Menzieshill farm on the western edge of the City was eventually acquired in 1955. The University Grants Committee stipulated that the Medical School was to be 'embedded' in the hospital; in other words, teaching, research and patient care were to be carried out under the same roof. Hence an entirely new type of teaching hospital was to emerge, the first of its kind in Scotland and in the UK.

In the past forty years Dundee has been transformed from a declining industrial city to one where teaching and research in medicine and the life sciences has given it, the City of Discovery, a world-wide reputation. Much of this transformation has arisen from the innovative nature and facilities embodied in the Ninewells project. Early signs of this trend were evident in the International Symposium at Queens College, Dundee (1961) which vividly foresaw the role which Ninewells Hospital and Medical School was later to play in the future of the new Dundee. It has been said that the success of Ninewells provided the critical mass which helped to attract funds for medical research in Dundee.

The Life Sciences sector in Dundee has developed an international reputation based on world class scientific research which is taking place within the University of Dundee. The sector now employs over 3900 people including 600 scientists from across the world. The recent announcement that Wyeth, one of the world's largest pharmaceutical companies, is basing its Translational Medical Research Collaboration (TMRC) in the city highlights the status Dundee now has in the Life Sciences sector. TMRC is now nearing completion on the Ninewells site, and with the adjacent Clinical Research Centre the number of scientists in Dundee continues to grow.

The objective of this Study, "Ninewells Revisited", is to tell the Ninewells part of the story from initial Brief to eventual completion and succeeding years of occupation. It is a story in which the working relationship between the Hospital Board, the University, the Design Team and the Scottish Office was a successful element, one which showed a sense of vision so often absent from publicly funded projects. In telling the story, a guiding principle has been to ensure that achievements and disappointments are given the same degree of objective scrutiny.

From consultations at the start of the Study with the staff working in the Hospital and Medical School it was clear that there was a surprising lack of understanding concerning the Brief and the principles on which the Design is based. The Study has therefore been structured as follows :--

The Brief and the Design	:	An explanation
Experience in use	:	Assessing the degree of staff satisfaction
Changes after occupation	:	How well have they been accommodated
The building operation	:	Why did it stumble at the first hurdle?

Fig 3 View from the north-west 1974

PROLOGUE

A study of how Ninewells has achieved its reputation as a centre of excellence in patient care, teaching and medical research reveals four key factors :-

1 The complete integration of the Medical School and Hospital.
2 Unified process of exploration in drafting the Brief and Design studies.
3 Commitment to the principle of adaptability and extendibility in planning.
4 The high quality of staff which Ninewells has attracted.

Large building projects have a tendency of going wrong for various reasons such as a poorly drafted Brief, a rush to get started on site, or incomplete contract documents. The Hospital Board and the University were well aware of this danger. Establishment of close working relationships among the participants from the start and allocation of time for architectural and functional studies to be prepared in tandem with drafting of the Brief ensured steady progress.

It was generally agreed that an objective account should be made of Ninewells Hospital and Medical School for two particular reasons. Firstly it is significant in regard to the advancement and teaching of modern medicine. Secondly it was the first new teaching hospital to be built in the UK for over 80 years. How it was conceived, how the Brief evolved, how the design process succeeded or failed, and whether an unusual form of contract was a success are therefore matters of considerable interest even after the passage of thirty years since commissioning.

It will be noted that the essential characteristic of the Ninewells solution illustrates how medical research and student teaching is brought closer to the care of the patient whilst at the same time retaining the Scottish tradition of a community based hospital

The task of preparing a well researched and documented Brief was formidable. Some decisions made during the briefing and early design stages might, with hindsight, appear to be imperfect, but at the time authoritative guidance was not available. Evolving medical, social, and technological developments were raising new questions, and undergraduate teaching was responding to new ideas in medical and nursing practice. This lack of relevant knowledge however had a certain advantage in so far as it enabled the Hospital Board, the University, and the Design Team to examine ideas and possible solutions from first principles. It is thus hardly surprising that the Brief and the Design did not necessarily follow the beaten path of perceived wisdom; indeed it would have been foolish to have done so.

Three characteristics of the Ninewells story remain in the collective memory, namely the successful way in which the Hospital Board and the University responded to the policy of the University Grants Committee for the Medical School, adoption of a unified planning structure embracing the Hospital Board, the University and the Design Team throughout the briefing and design stages, and the part played by Ninewells Hospital and Medical

School in the rise of Dundee to a place on the world stage of medical teaching and research.

Certain particular elements are apparent in the telling of the story :--

a) The interpretation of a new type of teaching hospital, in which student teaching, medical research, and patient care are brought closer together.
b) The close working relationship with the Nuffield Provincial Hospital Trust, focusing on research by John Musgrove and Brigadier J.D. Welch.
c) Finding new and better ways in which to achieve a compact scheme which nonetheless retains a degree of loose fit in areas of predictable growth.

Questions are sometimes asked about progress and the cost of Ninewells Hospital. Bearing in mind the innovative nature of the project, expectations of progress were, with hindsight, too optimistic. Increasing cost was partly inherent in the nature of the contract, and partly due to essential additions to the Brief subsequent to the appointment of the Contractor. The relatively poor performance of the Contractor added to the difficulties of estimating expected progress.

The crucial matter of adaptability in use since the commissioning in 1974 is central to this Study. Firstly it is necessary to understand the basis of design in anticipation of future expansion and in the implications of growth in staff and student numbers. Secondly, the near certainty of new specialties needing to be accommodated, and of changing medical and nursing practice. Following the retirement of Mr James Johnston Secretary to the Regional Hospital Board and Mr Robert Paton Project Administrator in 1982, subsequent developments proceeded with little regard to the principles underlying the Brief and the Design. Random additions of new buildings in spaces allocated for future expansion, or within the courtyards, have regrettably occurred.

To understand events in recent years it is necessary to review the salient features of the policies and principles upon which the Brief and the Design were based . The main focus in this Study has been on the wards, the operating theatres and the laboratories. The first part of the review is historical, concerned with explaining aspects of the Brief and the Design. The second part concerns experience and evaluation in use as reflected in discussions with members of staff; this has been a valuable exercise in learning directly from staff in the Hospital and Medical School ways in which the working environments meet or fall short of their expectations.

Preparation of a brief is never an easy task; for a project like Ninewells one has to look some years ahead to anticipate possible new developments in medical science, for example to the growth of robotics, to new diagnostic techniques, to increasing automation. It was in the nature of things that everyone involved with predicting future trends had to be aware of new knowledge, and to understand and observe the principles inherent in the design.

When existing experience is not in tune with current developments in medical and nursing practice and with a need for efficiency in use of resources of staff and of buildings, a search for new and relevant experience is vital. In consultations with John Musgrove and Brigadier Welch the need for new knowledge was apparent; as they said, *"old knowledge and untested beliefs often prevail in the mind of the user to the detriment of objective analysis"*. Sometimes one can be faced with broad statements in the preparation of a Brief, eg *"theatres should be of adequate size so as avoid overcrowding"*. In the field of work-study, a discipline in which Brigadier Welch had extensive experience, such statements are so vague as to be useless. In the preparation of the Ninewells Brief any tendency to the use such aspiring statements was kept in check.

Preparation of the Brief was divided, as normal, into two parts :-

a) Primary Brief : This covered functional requirements, staff and student numbers, preliminary estimates of space requirements, site development constraints, and a policy on provision for future growth.

b) Secondary Brief : This covered fixed and moveable equipment, specialist installations, safety measures, engineering services, operational policies, and central supply services.

Preparation of the Secondary Brief was a difficult task for both the Hospital Board, the Medical School, the Architect and the Services Engineer. It is not always appreciated that equipment is a determining factor in design of space, of engineering services and of the internal environment. Precise information needs to be shown on Room Data drawings. In many instances progress depended on manufacturers providing information on their equipment, (e.g. installation details, service connections, floor loading, floor finishes etc.) by the dates identified in the Design and in the Building programmes. The ingathering of this information was painfully slow.

THE BEGINNING

In 1949 the Secretary of State for Scotland approved in principle proposals by the Eastern Regional Hospital Board to close the existing Dundee Royal Infirmary and to concentrate all acute hospital services for Dundee 'on one site as near to the city centre as possible'. St Andrews University decided that its new Medical School should be built on the same site. Menzieshill farm on the western edge of the of the city was acquired in 1955. Sir Robert Matthew was appointed in 1956 as the architect for the project.

The intention was for the Hospital to contain all medical specialties required for a modern teaching hospital. It was assumed that the Hospital of about 900 beds, and the Medical School, would follow the convention at that time of being housed in separate buildings.

These assumptions were later abandoned because of two important decisions :--

By the Secretary of State for Scotland:	The bed complement of the hospital to be limited to a maximum of 720 beds. Subsequently the number was raised to 800 beds.
By the University Grants Committee:	The Medical School to be planned as an integral part of the Hospital, a concept which became known as 'embedding', meaning the closest possible relationship of the patient care function with the teaching and research functions.

The magical figure of 800 beds is said to be a hang-over from World War II when the custom was to disperse and to reduce the size of hospitals as much as possible in order to minimise casualties during enemy air raids. The explanation given at the time was that a hospital of more than 800 beds becomes 'inefficient'; no evidence was forthcoming to support such a view.

The Goodenough Committee Report of 1944 concluded that the number of beds in a teaching hospital should be related to the number of medical students; a ratio of ten students per bed was suggested. The rationale of this ratio was baffling. In terms of disturbance and hygiene procedures within a ward such a collection of students moving through a ward was considered unacceptable.

In January 1962 the Department of Health published a policy document entitled 'Hospital Plan for Scotland' in which, referring to Ninewells proposals, stated :- *"A new teaching hospital of 705 beds and medical school is to be built. It will replace the obsolete Dundee Royal Infirmary and, along with an enlarged Maryfield Hospital, will provide modern and additional patient accommodation and improved facilities for medical teaching".*

This policy statement was viewed by the Hospital Board and the University with disbelief. They enquired whether the University Grants Committee had agreed to a policy reversal from a unified teaching hospital on one site, to one split between two sites. The clinicians and the Joint Planning Committee were assured that the UGC had not reversed its policy. Mr James Deuchars,

Regional Board Architect, explained that the Maryfield site was too small and that the existing buildings had no lifts. The idea of a twin site was thus impractical. It was dropped, and a policy of a unified hospital and medical school on the Ninewells site was confirmed.

The idea of a twin site was later resurrected by the Department of Health by a proposal to extend the life of the old Dundee Royal Infirmary. In 1964 the Department decided that Orthopaedic surgery, Neurosurgery, and Plastic surgery were to be located in an upgraded Dundee Royal Infirmary. This surprising decision was opposed by Professor Donald Douglas, and his colleagues, not only because it ran counter to the concept of a new type of teaching hospital, but also because :-

a) Orthopaedics, Neurosurgery and Plastic surgery have a close functional relationship with each other and with the Department of Surgery
b) Orthopaedics, Neurosurgery and Plastic surgery are key components in the undergraduate and post-graduate teaching curriculum.
c) Modern medicine cannot be taught and practised in an obsolete hospital.

As Professor Douglas remarked, *"One cannot accept part of the Medical School to be 'un-embedded' at Dundee Royal Infirmary"*. Mr J K Johnston expressed astonishment at the proposed change of policy of September 1949 for a unified hospital and medical school on one site; he referred to the unknown costs of upgrading Dundee Royal Infirmary and those which would arise in the transfer of accommodation to Ninewells when DRI eventually closed. It was reported that the Scottish Office took the view that it would be unfair for Ninewells to have more beds than other teaching hospitals - if true, it was a curious and illogical observation.

The University emphasised that for a Medical School the number of beds and the type of patients should be determined primarily by the needs for the teaching of undergraduate and post-graduate students. The response of the University Grants Committee to the idea of a twin site, as Professor Hunter, a member of the UGC reported, was one of deep concern lest the concept of a new Medical School were to be set aside. In the event it was set aside, and the old Dundee Royal Infirmary continued in use for a further 25 years.

At the outset, a Joint Planning Committee was formed comprising members of the Hospital Board and the Medical Faculty of the University. From 1960 its chairman was Sir Lewis Robertson who was joined by Sir Malcolm Knox, Principal of St Andrews University (which embraced the Medical School in Dundee). The Committee was concerned with all matters of policy and with securing the earliest possible completion of the project. Its work was helped considerably by the participation of Andrew Hughes, Under-Secretary at the Department of Health, who was able in many instances to give immediate approval to well considered proposals.

Preparation of the Brief was a considerable task, one in which, as Sir Norman Graham of the Scottish Office, observed :-

"It calls for a proper appreciation of the functional requirements which the hospital is designed to serve. This seems to be part of the planning exercise that is inherently the most difficult and the one that is least understood. Here in Dundee, we believe that this responsibility has been discharged with a skill and thoroughness that we hope will serve as an example".

A Joint Technical Committee of the Hospital Board and University was set up to begin preparation of draft schedules of accommodation, to consider operational policies, and preliminary proposals from the users and from the Design Team. The work gave an initial impression of the composition and size of the project. The task raised many questions but the work progressed at a measured pace.

The world of medicine was changing and medical knowledge had come far since the time of Joseph Lister, James Young Simpson, and Alexander Fleming. There were however few examples of the impact of new knowledge on hospital and medical school design. It is probably fair to say that hospital design, to a large extent, had lost its way since Florence Nightingale laid down the rules :--

"No ward is in any sense a good ward in which the sick are not at all times supplied with pure air, light and due temperature. These are results to be obtained from hospital architecture, and not external design and appearance".

A bright note on the progress of hospital design at that time was seen in the work of the Nuffield Provincial Hospital Trust (1948-61). The Trust was doing important research in functional planning, for example on medical and surgical wards, on sterile supplies, on laboratory planning and on radiology departments. Its work brought ideas much closer to reality for hospital and medical school design. In the USA Gordon Friesen had adopted a new approach to hospital planning in a programme of hospitals for the United Mineworkers Union. It was based on a rational organisation of internal supply systems, and application of automation to the delivery of supplies to the point of use. These hospitals were also examples of neat and economical planning.

Responding to lack of sufficient objective information, and a near quiescent period of work, it was decided to form a small Study Team comprising Mr James Johnston, Dr James Hunter, and Dr Tom Sommerville. The Team became aware that it was not sensible to proceed with its work without an architect taking part; Alan Wightman joined the Team (it acquired the soubriquet 'The Quartet'). Its remit was of an exploratory nature embracing consultations with doctors, nurses and scientists and with John Musgrove and Brigadier Welch of the Nuffield Trust.

At this juncture an unexpected discussion Paper from the Architect appeared, entitled 'Factors influencing the height and bulk of building for the Hospital and Medical School'. It generated immediate interest on two counts. Firstly, it questioned the assumptions underlying the drafting of the Brief which had envisaged wards being housed in a tower block with clinical support and supply services located in a two-storey base, a common solution, for example, in the USA. Secondly, it underlined the importance of architectural/engineering studies running in tandem with the drafting of the Brief. As James Johnston observed, *"It is evident that the Paper makes a convincing case for a low rise solution; adoption of its conclusions would greatly enhance prospects of progress"*. Sir Malcolm Knox, recognising that a defining moment had been reached, convened a meeting of the University Court Committee on 21 October 1959. It was attended by Professor Robert Hunter, Professor Donald Douglas, Dr Tom Sommerville, J.K.Johnston, Sir Robert Matthew, Tom Spaven and Alan Wightman.

In addition to a review of progress, two items on the agenda were the Paper on the height and bulk of hospital buildings, and a proposal by Professor Hunter that John Musgrove, of the Nuffield Provincial Hospitals Trust, be formally invited to join the Design Team with a view to obtaining the benefit of his extensive experience in laboratory planning. Sir Robert stated his agreement with the conclusions of the Paper by Alan Wightman concerning the height and bulk of hospital buildings, and agreed to invite John Musgrove to play a central role in the compilation of the Brief and in the design of the laboratories. The meeting also welcomed Sir Robert's assurance that the Design Office of the Architect would be set up in Dundee under the leadership of Alan Wightman, with administrative responsibilities remaining in his Edinburgh office under Tom Spaven.

The scene was now set for making further progress. At a meeting of the Joint Planning Committee on 24 November 1959. an important statement was made :--

"In terms of establishing a broad impression of progress, the following statement is made concerning an outline of a possible programme :--

Tender accepted for the main buildings	*September 1963*
Handover of site to contractor	*October 1963*
Construction completed	*September 1968*

The period allowed for the approval of plans, costs and tenders must not be exceeded; it appears reasonable. In particular, no provision has been made for the possibility of negotiations between the Department and the UGC. The architect has agreed that the programme can be met although it provides the minimum possible time in each phase. The success of the programme will depend very largely on the architect who will require to concentrate substantial staff in his Dundee office, as Dundee must become the main centre of consultation as planning advances".

The Statement made no mention of a target for completion of the Secondary Brief and equipment schedules. Nevertheless it was a useful map of the road ahead and confirmed the role of the Architects' Dundee office in Hawkhill House. It also reflected confidence in the ongoing work, a notable characteristic being the close collaboration of the participants by means of a mix of frequent formal and informal meetings. The collaboration between the 'front line' of the Design Team in Hawkhill House and 'The Quartet' ensured a steady flow of ideas and draft proposals regarding the Brief and planning studies. In the words of J.K.Johnston, *"Mutual respect and understanding between the participants ensured good progress".*
The Design Report of May 1961 illustrated the kind of teamwork betwen Client and Design Team that ensured good progress. *"The carefully selected information within this report is exceptionally well written and illustrated. An excellent example of how an architect's report should be compiled".*
The Architects' Journal 6th September 1961.

THE CONCEPT

'Adaptability' and 'loose fit' are two characteristics of a response to uncertainty regarding future changes and future growth. In a prescient observation by Professor Hunter, he remarked *"It is a matter of extreme concern that the prospect of growth in medical research will be faster than anticipated"*. He was thus underlining the importance of these two characteristics.

Provision for a degree of adaptability and loose fit was made in four respects :--

a) A consistent and repetitive form of space planning, of structure, of floor loadings and of engineering services.
b) A planning solution which provided open ends to allow for horizontal expansion, particularly in the Medical School and the Main Ward block.
c) Where necessary, provision of a limited number of spaces required for specialised functions needing to have a higher degree of adaptability.
d) A form which allowed the optimum standardisation and ease of access in respect to the installation and maintenance of engineering services.

Schedules of room sizes were thus not the main element of the Primary Brief; the focus was on functions and relationships within a disciplined approach. In initial studies the main objective was to fuse dissimilar elements into a complex whole; it was thus necessary to identify key elements of the Hospital and Medical School, namely the critical zones within which there are distinctive characteristics in terms of function, occupation, access, safety etc.

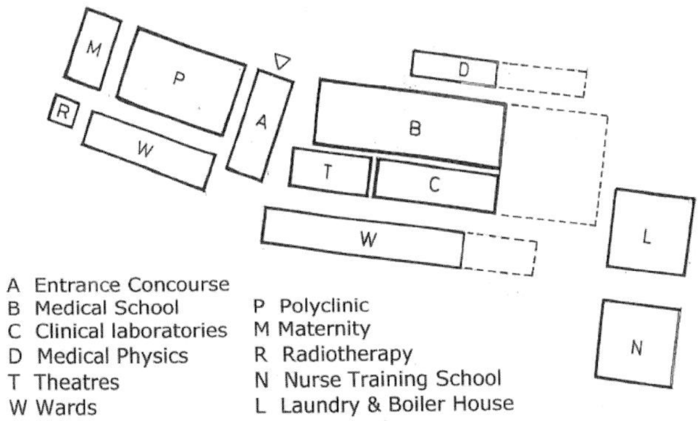

Fig 4 Zoning Diagram

Safety and ease of movement were the guiding principles for the planning of the circulation system. This was not just a matter of travel distances, but of clarity of plan and ease of movement between functionally related departments whilst taking care that patients and visitors to the Hospital do not inadvertently enter the Medical School. The main artery, the Hospital Street, and the secondary arteries originate from the heart of the circulation system, the Main Concourse.

Three particular objectives were :--

1) For reasons of safety, the movement of patients between wards and treatment facilities should be on the level, i.e. without the use of lifts.
2) Paraclinical departments in the Medical School to be capable of 100% expansion using the existing circulation pattern of the Medical School.
3) A degree of separation between differing kinds of internal traffic.

For reasons of security and staffing costs proliferation of external entrances was avoided. It was reckoned that it cost £600 a year to man a hospital entrance, and £2500 a year if manned 24 hours a day. (1962 costs). The Main Entrance was to be the point of arrival and departure for staff, walking patients, visitors to the Hospital and staff and students to the Medical School.

The sloping site provided an opportunity for vertical segregation of differing types of internal traffic, i.e. pedestrians, emergency admissions and supply traffic. Segregation is on three levels :--

Top	: Main entrance and routes linking wards and clinics.
Middle	: Emergency admissions and major treatment departments.
Bottom	: Supply and Services traffic.

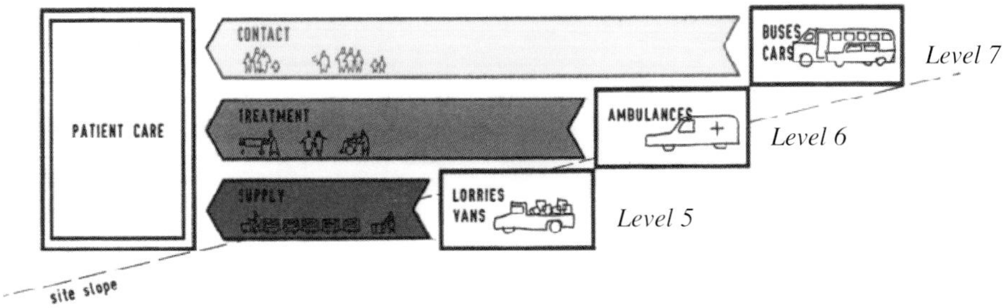

Fig 5 Traffic segregation

The advantages of exploring and illustrating design proposals by means of models are self-evident. Models are an important tool which help to visualise form and scale at each stage in the progress of the design work, and are especially helpful to a lay person when considering innovative proposals. For these reasons a model making facility was set up in Hawkhill House with a skilled model maker and photographer, Jim Eaton. It was an immensely useful, arguably essential, tool.

Fig 6 Model 1961 *Jim Eaton*

Fig 7 The completed building 1974. Aerial view from the East

To achieve reasonable compactness in a low rise scheme a degree of deep planning is necessary, a much used but misunderstood term. Deep planning as a concept is rightly criticised when a 'subterranean atmosphere' results owing to poor daylight and poor ventilation. Essentially, deep planning means the minimum possible frontage for a given size of space, whilst ensuring good daylight and ventilation. This has been achieved largely by means of a courtyard type of planning. To growing concern it is evident that some courtyards have been partially filled in. If infilling of courtyards was to continue in the manner of ad-hoc additions, the raison d'etre of this form of planning would be lost with predictable consequences.

The Medical School

The University Grant Committee's concept for 'embedding' of the Medical School raised the obvious question, "what is meant by the term embedding?" It became clear that delineation between the Medical School and Hospital would be somewhat fluid. As Professor Hunter (a member of the UGC) explained, an answer had to ensure a significant integration without loss of identity of the Medical School; it needed to be a balancing act, one which enabled clinicians, students and research workers to be close to the patients under one roof, with ease of communication between all involved.

The identity of the Medical School was to be seen in several ways:--

a) Clinical staff to be housed in the relevant ward unit.
b) Provision of accommodation for group teaching on the wards
c) Medical School staff to have an active presence in the Polyclinic.
d) Medical School and Hospital laboratories planned as a unified whole.
e) Communal spaces shared by staff in the Hospital and Medical School.
f) The provision of a Joint Clinical Investigation Unit.

Professor Hunter and Dr Tom Sommerville emphasized the need for a 'close fit' between the patient care and the teaching functions, as reflected for example in the provision of Demonstration and Tutorial rooms in each ward unit; a visible aspect of the concept of embedding.

This provision served two purposes:-

- The need to foster the tutorial method of student teaching in small groups
- Reduction in time spent by students attending systematic lectures

The identity of the Medical School is first seen at its entry from within the Main Concourse and in locations specific to the Medical School. It is to be seen by what Professor Pippard refers to as 'the heart' of the Medical School, namely the Library, the lecture theatres and the Ian Lowe centre. With the growing recognition of this new type of teaching hospital, applications from students keen to train in medicine have risen over the past 30 years from 110 to 154.

There has been a suggestion that the existing provision for future expansion of the Library could be used for group teaching of medical students. The concept of embedding meant that teaching should be conducted as close to patient care as possible, hence the location 'in a clinical atmosphere' of Demonstration and Treatment Rooms on each Ward Unit. The provision for a planned expansion of the Library was a requirement of the University Grants Committee on the evidence of steady growth of university libraries. It is difficult to see how such a suggestion could comply with the concept.

That this concept of embedding for a Teaching Hospital has been adopted is mainly due to the farsighted policy of the University Grants Committee and its ready acceptance by the Joint Planning Committee.

GROWTH AND CHANGE

The architectural solution had to achieve a balance between a reasonable degree of compactness and a degree of 'loose fit' to allow for small changes in the use and growth of space. As already noted, two important characteristics of a low-rise scheme are ease of movement and a means of providing for future changes. When future changes are considered, two questions need careful consideration :-

a) Does the proposed change nullify the initial provisions for future growth ?
b) How would the proposed change impact on existing accommodation ?

Priority for provision for future expansion was identified as the diagnostic and research laboratories, the two ward blocks, the polyclinic and student facilities in the Medical School. The provision is reflected in four main areas:--(fig 9)

1) Paraclinical & Research laboratories, to be able to expand eastwards from two open ends along the contours of the site. The University Grants Committee required the laboratory complex of the Medical School to have provision for 100% expansion.
2) The Main Ward block to be able to expand eastwards to provide for three new 48-bed ward units
3) The West Ward Block to be able to expand vertically by means of an additional storey.
4) The Library Block to be able to expand northwards by one structural unit of space.

The Brief required provision for about 50% expansion in the Polyclinic; this has been met by provision for an additional partial storey (fig 8). In respect of future vertical expansion the structural design allowed for a lightweight form of dry construction for the additional storey.

Fig 8 Polyclinic: Planned future expansion on level 8

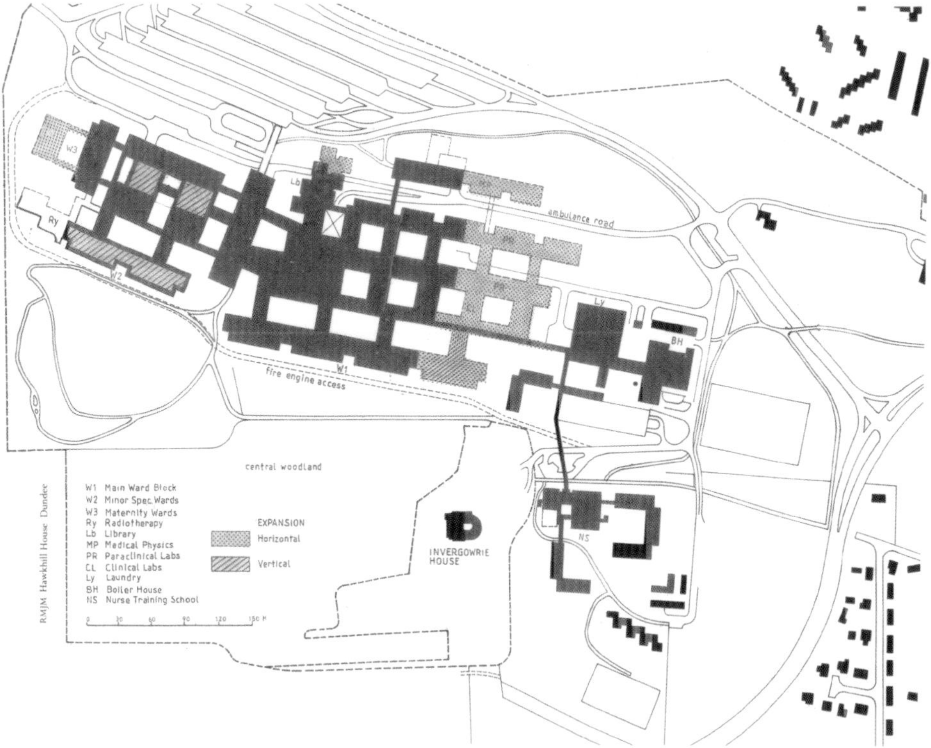

Fig 9 Future Expansion as planned 1964 (highlighted in blue)

Fig 10 Aerial view of completed project showing how the concourse block relates to the two ward blocks

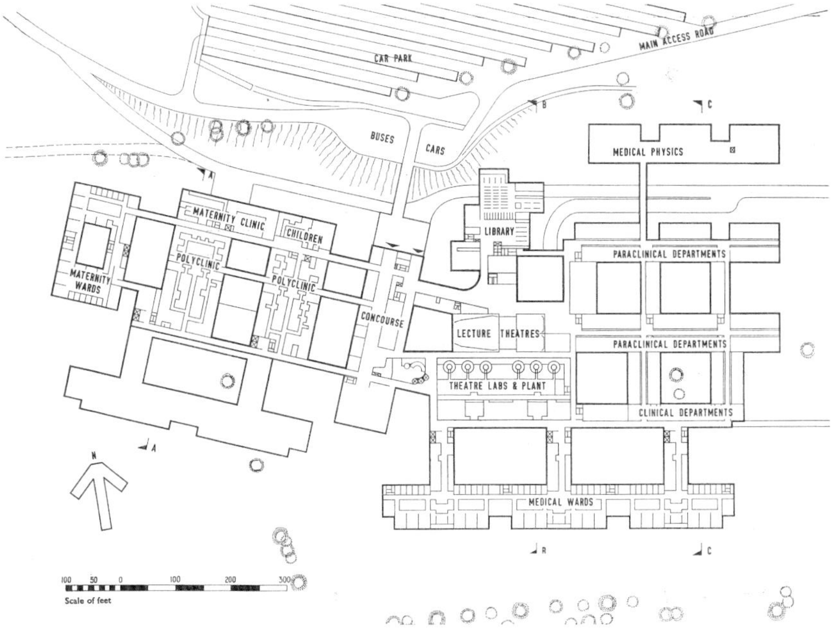

Fig 11 General Floor Plan Concourse Level 7

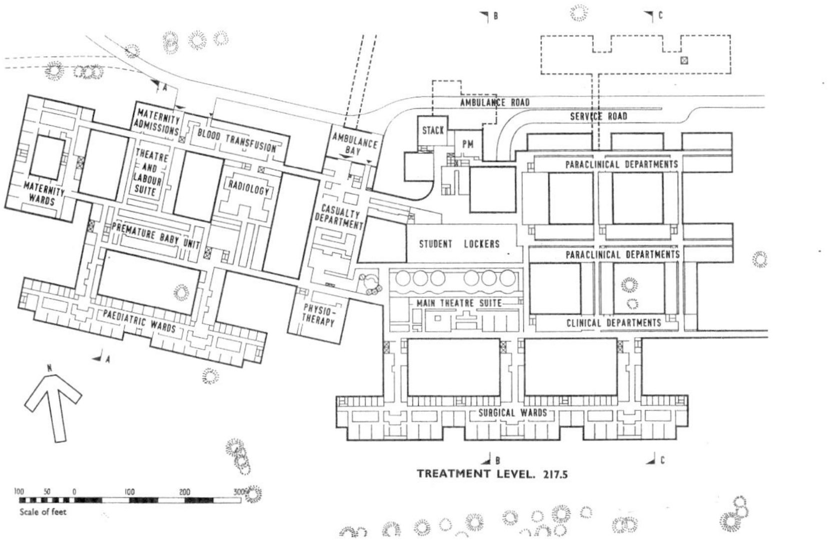

Fig 12 General floor plan Treatment Level 6

TYPICAL MEDICAL & SURGICAL WARD UNIT

The fact that the Nightingale ward had been the prevailing pattern of ward design for such a long time is remarkable. Its origins can be traced to the time of the Crimean War when Florence Nightingale's inspired views as a nurse and Isambard Kingdom Brunel's design skills as an engineer and architect came together in 1855 at a time of national crisis. Brunel's design of a 'pavilion' type of ward reflected their convictions as to the need for good ventilation and good sanitary facilities, which included proper drainage and flushing toilets. The design was so successful that it was the model for what became known as the 'Nightingale ward'.

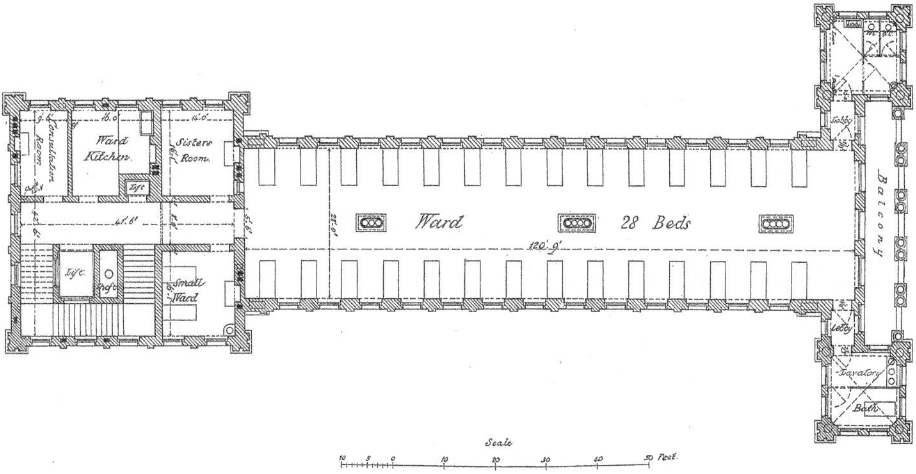

Fig 13 St Thomas's Hospital : original Nightingale ward 1868

With ceiling heights of 3.60 metres and windows on opposite walls, natural cross ventilation was effective in helping to minimise air-borne infection; the 'quick blow-through' was one of the ward sister's ready weapons in the fight against hospital acquired infection. In the post-war years a search for a replacement of the Nightingale ward was prompted partly by the 'military' characteristics of its layout, but much more so by the fact that the high dependency end of the ward was at its entrance where there is most traffic and noise.

There was a perception that a modest degree of privacy could be achieved by sub-division of the Nightingale ward similar to that adopted in the Rigs Hospital in Copenhagen where the layout of the beds is parallel to the external walls and grouped in the form of open bays. This arrangement also helped to simplify the ventilation design.

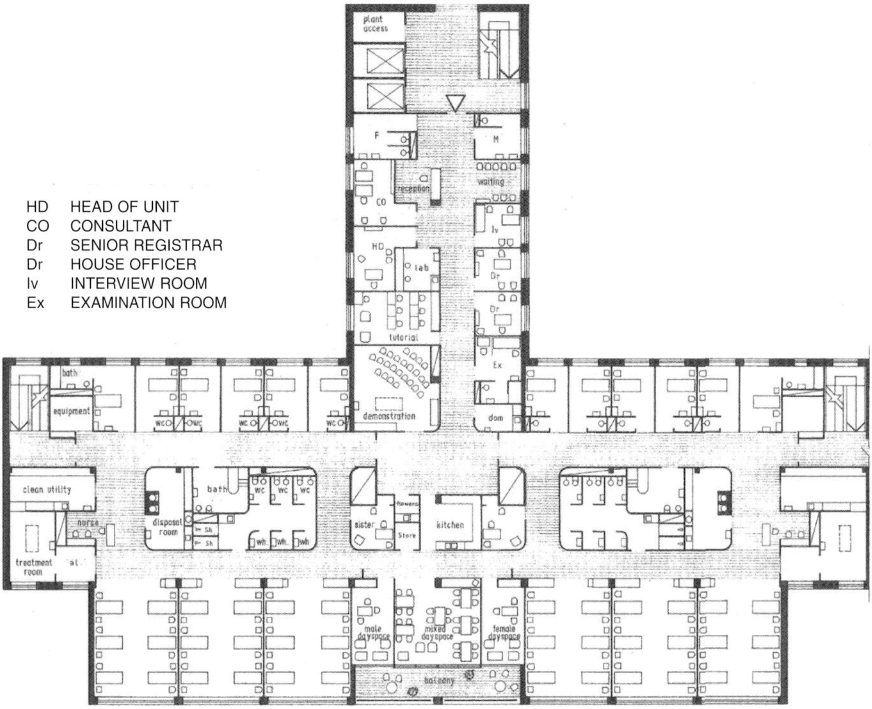

Fig 14 Typical 48-bed Ward Unit,

Wards of single rooms, the norm in America and several European countries, may offer some privacy, but visual supervision by the nurses, essential for safety reasons, is made more difficult, especially at night. Imagine the night nurse on a 24 bed ward gently opening 24 doors for a keek to see whether a patient is disturbed, has fallen out of bed, or indeed, gone missing. Except in the case of barrier nursing, there was no clinical evidence that adoption of wards of single rooms, per se, reduced the incidence of hospital acquired infection.

Some patients in single rooms seem to experience a sense of isolation and occasionally, as nurses have observed, become depressed. When a patient asks for the room door to be left open this would appear to indicate a subliminal preference to see and hear the daily bustle of work on the ward, and so relieve boredom. On a visit to the USA by representatives of the Department of Health and two members of the Ninewells team, many examples were seen of single rooms in hospital wards where the doors were kept open during the day at the request of the patient.

Fig 15 Main Ward Block 1974 - garden frontage

Apart from questions of safety, it is considered that more nurses would be needed if wards were to be based primarily on single rooms. Hence the decision was adopted for the standard Ninewells ward to contain three open bays each of 6 beds, with six single rooms for infected cases, the dying, the noisy, and those with a particular need for rest and quiet. If the open bays are noisy, for example where there is 'non-stop TV', then one can understand a patient's desire to be in a single room. The decision for TV to be located in the central day space was seen as a significant benefit both for patients and staff. In the views expressed by doctors and nurses, the typical medical and surgical ward with its open bays and day spaces works well for patients, nurses and doctors.

To minimise the risk of hospital acquired infection, five policy statements were adopted on the recommendation of Professor Robert Hunter and of Dr Tom Sommerville :-

- A detailed prescription for daily cleaning and hygiene to be prepared as part of a drive for rigorous infection control to be overseen by the ward sister who would have an enhanced authority to enforce necessary standards of hygiene.

- To minimise procedures and traffic at the bedside, Treatment Rooms to be provided in each ward designed to the standard of a minor theatre, and located next to the Nurses Station.

- No group teaching around each bed. This was to be done in the Tutorial and Demonstration Rooms in each Ward Unit

- Bed spacing to be in accordance with the recommendations of the Cohen Committee (1959), namely at 8 foot centres.

- An appropriate standard of mechanical ventilation to be provided.

The 48-bed T-shaped Ward Unit (Fig 14), with a Sister in charge of each 24-bed ward, was adopted for three principal reasons:-

a) The high dependency ends of the two wards are remote from the entrance.
b) The open bays are relatively free of traffic and allow for good observation.
c) The clinical staff would be accommodated in the stem of the Ward Unit along with the Demonstration Room and the Tutorial Room.

There is a small measure of flexibility in use of the Ward Unit; for example, by single rooms in one ward overflowing into single rooms of the adjacent ward. Partly for reasons of security and to assist visitors, it was decided that each Ward Unit would be overseen at its entrance by a ward clerkess.

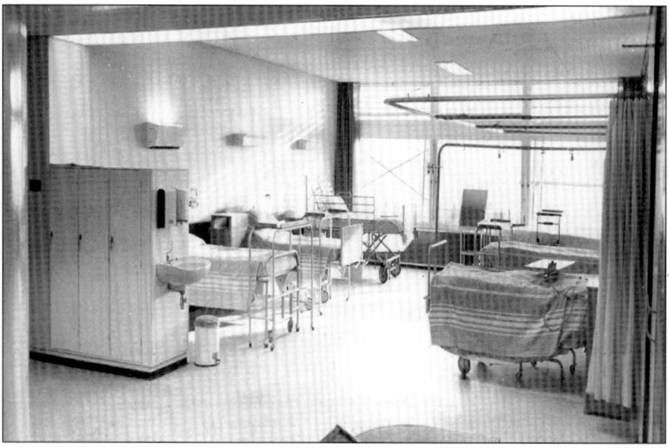

Fig 16 mock-up - 6-bed bay in a typical ward

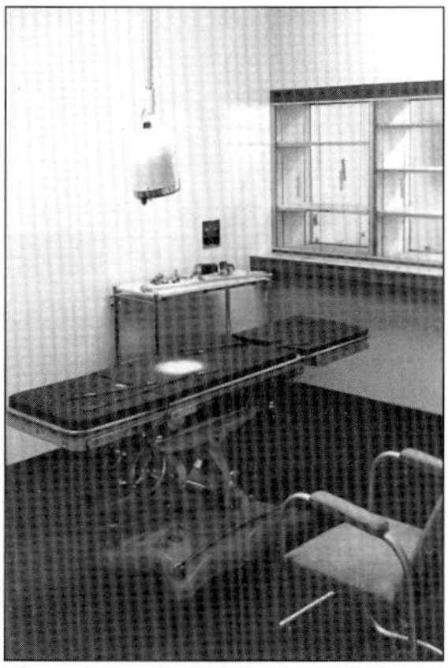

Fig 17 mock-up Ward Treatment Room

It is sometimes assumed that privacy in the wards would be improved if each bay had its own toilet and shower. This may have merit where the bed bays open directly off a main corridor serving several wards. From a patient's viewpoint toilets located within a 6-bed bay is an unpleasant arrangement, partly due to plumbing noise. There are also significant extra costs arising from dispersed plumbing, and the need for plumbers to enter bed areas when maintenance work is necessary. For these reasons there was general agreement to locate toilets and showers in a central core within each ward. When maintenance to toilets and showers is necessary, disturbance within the bed area is avoided. It is also self-evident that this arrangement is more economical than one based on dispersed plumbing. The grouping also allows for a small measure of flexibility in use within a Ward Unit.

The Brief followed the established policy of early ambulation requiring suitable day-rooms in each ward unit. Nursing opinion supported its division into a main space shared by men and women where meals are taken, and two small and quiet spaces, one for women, the other for men. Despite a steady reduction in the length of stay for patients, medical opinion continued to support the policy of progressive self-help in the interests of patients and nurses. In later years a search for more office space on the wards without encroaching on patient and teaching space has not been successful. In some wards tutorial rooms have become offices and it is said that some treatment rooms are now little used as such.

It was reckoned that if the planning of the typical ward was to be based mainly on single rooms there would be about an 18% increase in the cost of building. In the design studies it was also found that beds in open bays occupy 90 sq ft per bed, whereas beds in single rooms occupy 120 sq ft per bed.

The trend towards deep planning as applied to typical medical and surgical wards can be illustrated by the overall depths of the wards as shown in the following examples :--

Nightingale ward 28 feet (8.50m)	Jonkoping, Sweden 102 feet (31.10m)
St Thomas, London 42 feet (12 .90m)	Falkirk, Scotland 90 feet (27.40m)
Musgrave Park, Belfast 52 feet (15.86m))	Ninewells Dundee 78 feet (23.80m)

A measure of compactness relating to the frontage of a typical Ward Unit is illustrated in the following analysis (area figures represent sq feet):--

	Number of beds	Gross area ward unit	Gross area per bed	Number of beds per 10 ft run of building
St Thomas's	28	7,960	284	1.86
Cardiff	32	11,060	346	1.68
Ninewells	48	15,730	328	2.33

The Joint Planning Committee decided that a 24 bed 'stand-by' ward was necessary for use in emergencies, and to enable rotational cleaning and redecorating of the wards. For no clear reason it was not approved by the Department of Health.

MAIN THEATRE SUITE

In the past, the custom had been to provide operating theatres in the form of twin suites with shared facilities. For reasons of strict aseptic control, the Brief rejected this custom in favour of single theatres each with its own ancillary facilities and ventilation plant. Such an arrangement has the merit of avoiding a mirror image in the layout of each theatre.

In order to improve aseptic control, the Professor of Surgery Sir Donald Douglas advocated a substantial reduction in the number of people and equipment within the theatre. Accordingly, viewing windows were provided in the domed ceiling of each theatre in the belief that medical and nursing students and technicians needed to have a total view of theatre activity; it seems that they were not much used and have now been screened off. An important innovation was the separation of traffic, i.e. medical staff and patients entering via the 'Access' and 'Clean' corridors, with disposal items for the laundry or incineration exiting via the 'Dirty' corridor.

Professor Douglas referred to the records which show that wound infection had more than doubled since the last War, a fact which related to increased turnover, to overcrowding and overuse of theatres. He explained, *"As a matter of principle, the aim must be to give every case the conditions and inherent advantages of the first case, to observe a safe maximum for each case load, and that proper control of infection was the determining principle in deciding the number of theatres, not the case loads"*. The Joint Planning Committee decided that the Main Theatre Suite should consist of seven theatres with six theatres in continuous use, the seventh being held for emergencies and for allowing thorough cleaning of theatres by rotation. To the dismay of the Committee and of the surgeons and theatre staff the Department of Health gave approval for only six theatres.

To ensure that the required standard of care for patients and theatre staff was achieved, the Brief included the following accommodation :--

a) A Reception Ward was to be provided within the Theatre Suite to which a patient is brought from his/her ward.
b) A Recovery Ward was to be provided within the Theatre Suite in which a patient remains under observation until safe to return to the ward.
c) For reasons of safety, theatres were to be located on the same floor level as their related wards, thus avoiding transfer of a patient by a lift.
d) The Anaesthetic Department to be incorporated in the Main Theatre Suite with its own laboratory.

Of the six theatres in the Suite, four were for routine surgery, the other two allocated for gynaecology and paediatrics. The Brief stated *"Of the four theatres available for routine work, it is intended that only three should be used in any one day, the fourth being closed in rotation for thorough cleaning and service maintenance"*.

Professor Douglas, referring to the strong case for the Accident & Emergency Service to be located at Ninewells along with the Departments of Orthopaedic Surgery, Neurosurgery and Plastic Surgery, explained that these disciplines are closely related and form part of the teaching curriculum. To the surprise of the Hospital Board and the University, the Department of Health decided all these departments were to be located in the Dundee Royal Infirmary. Mr Johnston questioned the sense of this decision in view of substantial inadequacies of an obsolete hospital and significant costs arising from its likely closure in the short term.

The impact of closure of Dundee Royal Infirmary in 1998 and the transfer of its surgical facilities to Ninewells resulted in considerable changes within the Main Theatre Suite, which had to accommodate orthopaedic surgery in two of its theatres. In the view of Mr Robert Wood, consultant surgeon, *"the removal from general surgery of 30 beds and a seventh theatre not being built made a significant difference, not only in dealing with acute case loads, but of reducing waiting times."*

In general terms, the design of the Theatre Suite is regarded by the surgeons and nurses as excellent, and has been able to adapt to these changes by working to capacity and relinquishing evening and weekend 'down time'.

Some 50% of surgical procedures are now performed laparoscopically (a technique that was pioneered in Dundee by Sir Alfred Cuschieri) to the benefit of wound healing and reducing the length of stay in hospital.

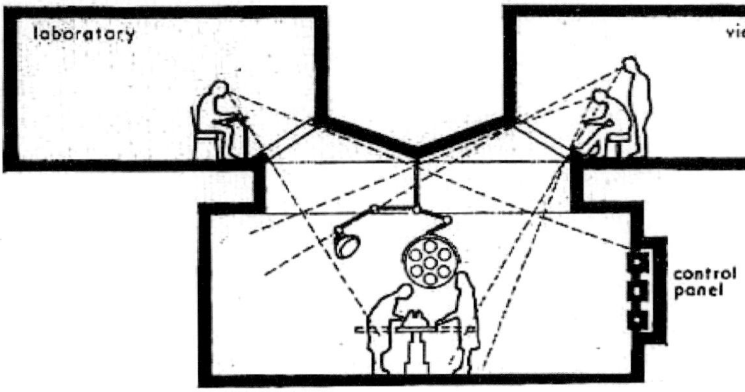

a) Section

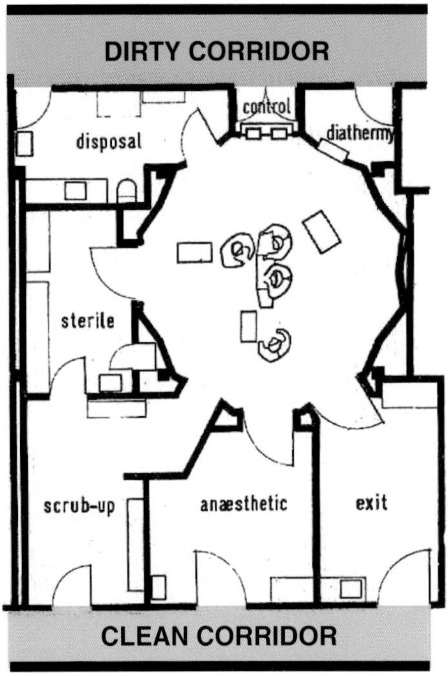

b) Plan

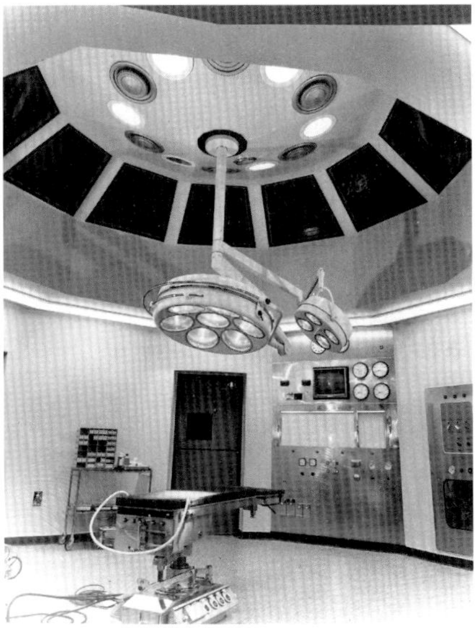

c) Interior view

Fig 18 Typical operating theatre

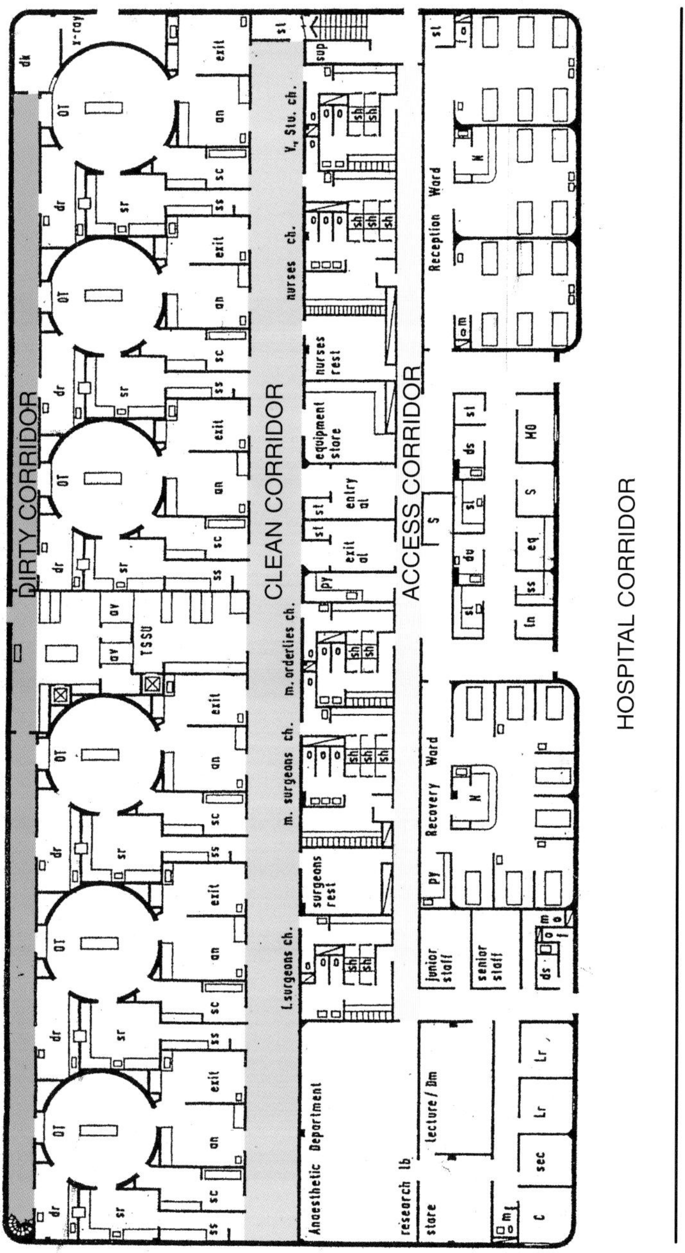

Fig 19 The Main Theatre Suite and Anaesthetic Department

LABORATORY DESIGN

The high cost of engineering services in medical and scientific laboratories requires a disciplined approach to laboratory design in two important respects :-

1) Provision of standard laboratory units which can be extended lineally along the spine corridor to which they are connected.
2) In order to minimise the cost of sub-mains along the spine, the frontage of a standard unit to be kept as small as possible.

For these reasons the laboratory accommodation in the Medical School was placed to enable expansion to take place eastwards along the site contours. Thus the paraclinical laboratories would be able to grow whilst remaining an integral part of the Medical School.

This approach to laboratory design was based on research work of John Musgrove at the Nuffield Trust. In regards to demands for 'flexibility' one recalls his words:-

> *"Laboratories tailor-made to the demands of an individual will result in a total loss of flexibility and costs would soon escalate. Generally speaking, people are more flexible than buildings. It is perfectly feasible to provide standard laboratories to suit a range of disciplines".*

Some unease was expressed at the apparently rigid nature of the structural / planning grid in two respects :--

a) The width of the standard bay was seen to be too tight
b) The structural grid was not amenable to larger groupings of linked spaces

Early requests began to appear for a less rigid basis of space planning in order to provide 'flexibility' to take account of differing sizes of laboratories.

John Musgrove explained that the ergonomics of laboratory planning had been subject to extensive research which showed that standard bays based on a frontage of 3.60 metres for science and medical laboratories satisfied most requirements. He stressed that the economics of laboratory design depends on the standardisation of structure and of services to the optimum extent together with and the use of non-load-bearing partitions. As he expressed it, *"standardisation is the key by which one can turn the process of space planning on its head, by allocating people to spaces rather that spaces to people"*. This approach depends of course on a sensible degree of space planning based on the choice for the structural grid.

With standard bays of 3.60 metres, the degree of adaptability provides, for example, laboratories of a single bay with or without a study cubicle, double or triple bay, and a professorial suite (fig 20).

To allow for growth in research work, the University Grants Committee approved provision of 17.5% of unallocated space in the Brief ; an imaginative decision. Increasing automation in laboratory work is resulting in high levels of heat which has meant installation of cooling equipment in several laboratories. Certain procedures and new specialist equipment have tended to need larger laboratories with island benches. Where this has been necessary, the adaptation has been skillfully carried out. With the rapid growth of medical research it is apparent that the John Musgrove principles of laboratory design have proved to be a success.

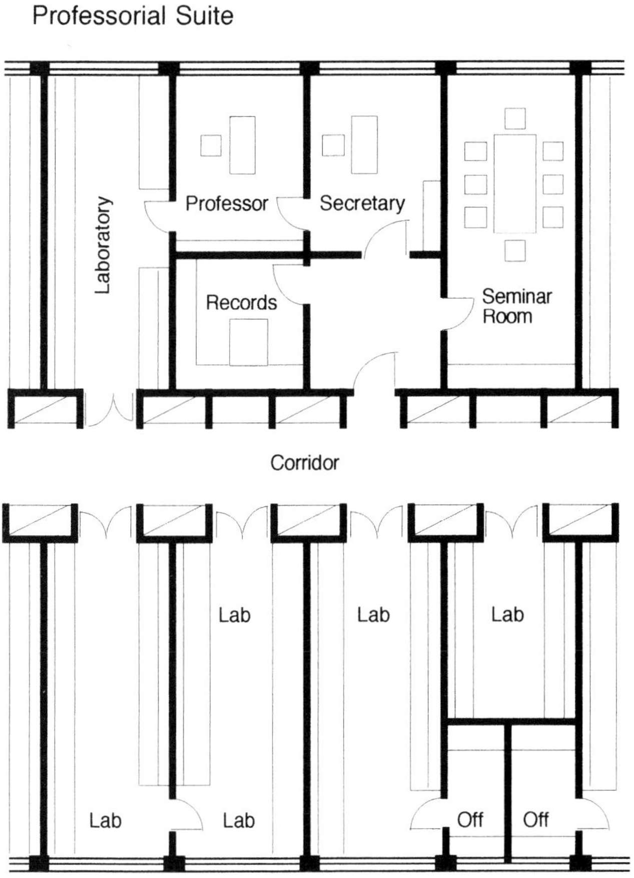

Fig 20 Laboratory complex: an example of flexible planning

ENGINEERING SERVICES

Whereas the importance of mechanical and electrical services in hospitals was well recognised at the time of formulating the Brief, as Sean Mulcahy had observed in the past the provision tended to be of a dispersed and minimal nature, of providing a little of everything, everywhere. Under the influence of the work of Gordon Friesen in America and the experience of the Danish Consultants Steensen, Varming & Mulcahy (SVM), a careful policy of centralising routine services was adopted where it was beneficial to do so. Design of engineering services was determined by necessary environmental standards, comfort, infection control, air freshness, and staff and patient safety.

Provision of a Piped Services Street, in the experience of SVM a rare feature in highly serviced buildings, was a key element in facilitating future changes and in relative ease of routine maintenance. Located at the lowest level in the hospital complex it was intended for the exclusive use of maintenance staff.

Fig 21
Piped Services Street

Steensen, Varming & Mulcahy aimed to provide a degree of flexibility generally. The design of the structure took account of ease of installation and access to bench services; there are no load-bearing walls, no downstand beams, a consistent design of the floor structure, with bench services planned to run above floor level.

The incidence of cross-infection was considered at the time to be largely concerned with poor ventilation; hence the need to ensure adequate air movement from dirty and odour-generating areas to where it is extracted, using an appropriate degree of dilution. Generally air movement is by means of mechanical ventilation, for example air in wards is extracted via the central core. Cool air conditioning is limited to specific areas such as theatres and certain laboratories where heat generating equipment is installed.

With instrument sterilisation located in a Central Sterile Supply department, it was decided policy on Dr Sommerville's advice that instruments used in the Animal House (located at the lowest level of the Medical School) must never be sent to the CSSD. If this were allowed to happen; he stated :-
"whilst high standards using modern sterilising equipment are achievable, one incidence of failure could have a catastrophic outcome".

STUDENT RESIDENCES

The University Grants Committee in its publications laid down space standards for student residences. Study-bedrooms for example were to be 110 sq.feet. This was based on an assumption that study bedrooms, bathrooms, kitchens and dining space would each be opening directly off a common corridor serving the study-bedrooms. Studies and consultations with nursing staff suggested an alternative of 4-person student flats to be planned within a permissible area of 440 sq feet, to provide four study bedrooms, a living room, a bathroom, and a kitchenette. The flats are well liked. An identical solution was adopted for the 28 medical student flats. The Brief also called for a small proportion of bed-sits.

Design of the bathrooms revolved around the issue of baths versus showers. A 'good soak in a bath after a heavy day' was well supported. Miss McNaught, Nursing Advisor to the Department of Health, suggested that the nurses should be invited to vote on the issue. The outcome of the vote was 86% in favour of showers.

There was a request from the nurses to be able to enjoy the therapeutic benefit of a Jacuzzi. Instead two private benefactors, the Matthew Trust and the ICL Trustees, provided the funds for the construction of a swimming pool within the Nurse Training School.

Fig 22 Student Residences & Nurse Training School 1974

FULL-SCALE MOCK-UPS

For reasons arising from new ideas emerging in the briefing and design stages, a proposal to construct full-scale mock-ups of selected elements of the Hospital and Medical School was readily agreed by the Department of Health. The Department provided a special budget of £64,000 (1961 prices). Selection focused on those elements which, to a significant degree, were innovative or were responding to particular features in the Brief.

The programme was planned in three stages:-

Programme 1
Typical Ward Unit : 6-bed bay, a single room, and central lavatory core
Dirty and Clean Utility Rooms
Treatment Room
Maternity - Standard delivery room
Residences - Study bedroom and sitting room
Programme 2
Standard Operating Theatre, with ancillary accommodation
Single Ward in the Joint Clinical Investigation Unit
Standard Laboratory Unit
Standard Consultation Suite in the Outpatient Department
Programme 3
Laboratory planning
Standard fitments, and fume cupboard.

Space planning, equipment, lighting, built-in fittings, etc were demonstrated as if in a real situation. Furniture, equipment and lighting were installed in each of the demonstrations and typical procedures tested. In the fully-equipped mock-up theatre Professor Douglas and his team even carried out a mock operation. It was a valuable experiment in a near-real 'piece of theatre'.

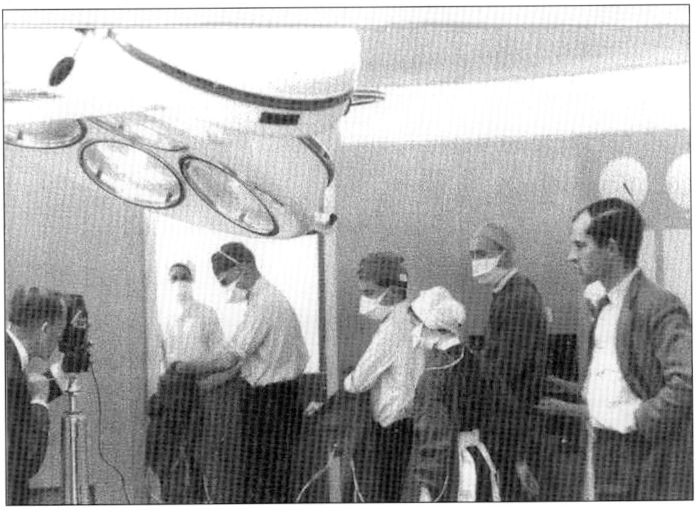

Fig 23 Professor Douglas simulating an operation in a mock-up of a typical theatre

Fig 24 Temporary building for full-scale mock-ups

Daylight penetration and artificial lighting were measured, various designs of windows and doors were tested, and wall and ceiling finishes illustrated. Programme One was completed in September 1963. Programmes Two and Three followed in May 1964. Over 600 people visited the demonstrations, and valuable information was obtained from the responses. A visiting group of nurses expressed particular interest in the 48-bed ward unit which they considered to be the natural successor to the Nighingale ward, being a balance between patient privacy and good nurse observation, especially at night.

Andrew Hughes of the Department of Health was very impressed with the demonstrations, saying that there are many instances where full-scale mock-ups should form part of the design process. With important lessons learned and many perceptive observations, the design programme and general progress gained immense benefit from the demonstrations. Most of the modifications which arose concerned matters of detail, in many instances important detail. The stage was then set for final design to proceed on a firmer basis.

Two Additions to the Brief

During the course of building, solutions to two necessary additions to the Brief were needed, namely provision for an increase of 60% in the intake of medical students required by the University Grants Committee, and the incorporation of a Radiotherapy Department as an integral part of the Hospital. The location and planning of this Department presented certain problems in respect of internal access from within the hospital and of adequate protection against radiation hazards. The Regional Physicist, Mr MacKenzie, approved the proposed solution in respect to its location, access, and radiation protection.

ADAPTABILITY IN USE

Adaptability and provision for future expansion were central to the formulation of the Brief and throughout the design stages. There appears to be general agreement that in the years since occupation 30 years ago, the design of the Hospital and Medical School has stood up reasonably well to the process of change.

To quote Mr Robert Wood, Consultant Surgeon :

> *"The integration of Hospital and Medical School is an outstanding success. In addition, the amount of unallocated space which was incorporated in the design has been of huge assistance in coping with some of the unforeseeable changes which have occurred so that the large number of brilliant scientists could move in".*

Ninewells has had to adapt to the transfer of services from other hospitals in Dundee, in particular the Royal Infirmary (DRI) and Kings Cross Hospital which at the time of closure had a combined complement of some 350 beds. The bed complement at Ninewells has increased from the original 753 to 888, an increase of just 135 beds. Despite this apparent reduction in the need for beds within the Dundee Hospitals, there has been a substantial escalation in the annual number of in-patients from 22,000 in the 1980s to 56,658 in 2006. Numbers of emergency medical admissions have also risen steeply in recent years.

Attempts to cope with this unprecedented situation (often referred to as the 'big squeeze') have included :-

a) Reducing the length of stay of patients whenever possible.
b) Increasing the proportion of day cases.
c) Increasing the number of beds in some wards from 24 to 30 beds.
d) Accommodating patients ('boarders') in whatever wards have spare beds irrespective of the specialty.
e) Conversion of some wards in order to accommodate both male and female patients with consequent erosion of day space and a worrying strain on the nurses in respect of the bathing and toilet facilities shared by both sexes.

As Professor Douglas and JK Johnston remarked, this regrettable situation was foreseeable when the policy of a joint site was abandoned and DRI given an extended life.

Ian Lowe Centre

A popular social space has been skillfully created by means of an elegant glazed atrium in a former courtyard. It is for the use both of staff and students in the Medical School and the Hospital.

Fig 25 The Ian Lowe Centre *AW*

The concourse

The Main Concourse has an affinity with a transit lounge in an airport. It was originally intended as a relatively calm space enlivened by murals, posters and tapestries to add interest and colour (the relationship between art and medicine has a long history). Later additions of small shops and a café have however enhanced its welcoming character, so different from typical Victorian hospitals with their over-bearing and lofty entrances.

Fig 26 The Main Concourse

Central Sterile Services Department (CSSD)

A combination of becoming a regional service and changing standards necessitated relocation of this department from within the hospital to a new building on the site of the hockey pitch at the east side of the hospital, and a change of name to Sterile Services Department (SSD).

Kitchen

To ensure high standards at reasonable cost, it was decided policy that meals are to be prepared in-house. In recent years the central kitchen has undergone substantial improvements. Patients and staff have commented favourably on the high quality, presentation, and delivery of healthy meals.

Research Centres

Two new stand-alone research centres have recently been built on the Ninewells site The recently opened Clinical Research Centre contains a new type of scanner, known as a PET-CT scanner, seen as a hugely significant facility for NHS Tayside and for the University of Dundee. In the Translational Medical Research Collaboration (TMRC), important studies are being carried out into the translation of basic scientific and clinical research into new drug discoveries. Both research centres greatly enhance the international reputation of Dundee University and its Medical School.

Main Ward Block

Provision was made in the initial Design Report for future expansion of the Main Ward Block (fig 9). This was intended to allow for three 48-bed Ward Units, one 24-bed ward providing temporary accommodation for a ward undergoing redecoration or a sudden emergency. The net increase in bed capacity of the hospital would thus have been 120 beds. The closure of Kings Cross Hospital and its relocation to Ninewells has prevented this planned expansion of the Main Ward Block.

Balconies in the Ward Units reflect the belief of Florence Nightingale that patients need to smell the fresh air outwith the confines of the ward, if only for brief moments. Hence the balconies in a typical Ninewells ward were regarded as an integral part of the ward design, intended to allow patients to benefit from the therapeutic value of sunshine and external views across the Tay.

Balconies can also be used to grow container plants which can provide colour and texture for patients and nurses to enjoy. From an architectural viewpoint, balconies provide important modelling to an otherwise uninteresting flat facade (Fig 15). It is regrettable that many of the balconies in the Ward Units have been removed.

DUNDEE ROYAL INFIRMARY

Fig 27 Dundee Royal Infirmary circa 1970 *RG*

At the time of preparing the Brief there was uncertainty as to the future of Dundee Royal Infirmary. Local opposition to its closure was evident. Whether this was a primary factor in the Secretary of State's decision for the Accident & Emergency Service to be located at DRI along with the departments of Orthopaedics, Neurosurgery and Plastic Surgery is not known. Despite firm opinions expressed by the Joint Planning Committee against the continued use of this obsolete hospital, the outcome meant that no provision, other than space for future expansion, was included in the Ninewells Brief.

Medical opinion considered that the operation of a split of vital services to patients arriving at the Accident & Emergency service at Dundee Royal Infirmary was fraught with potential danger. It was said that behind the decision by the Department of Health not to close Dundee Royal Infirmary was a belief that its closure would result in 'unfairness in the allocation of beds as between Ninewells and other teaching hospitals'. The relevance of this observation was obscure. It was also suggested that an increase in the number of beds at Ninewells would lessen efficiency, an opinion not shared by the Joint Planning Committee and not substantiated by available evidence.

The experience of the clinicians confirmed the mistake of locating the Accident & Emergency Service at Dundee Royal Infirmary. As one doctor observed, *"it is an anachronism for DRI to have an Accident & Emergency Service but no intensive care unit attached to it"*.

But it was more than that :--

a) The split in closely related surgical services could be putting lives at risk when cases needing immediate surgery had to be rushed to Ninewells

b) Elements of the Medical School would be detached at DRI so contravening the settled UGC policy of embedding the Medical School in Ninewells Hospital.

c) The old Victorian Infirmary was, in the view of the University Grants Committee, unsuitable for the practice and teaching of modern medicine (In the 'Hospital Plan for Scotland 1962', Dundee Royal Infirmary was described as 'obsolete').

In January 1994 it was decided to close Dundee Royal Infirmary, and its functions transferred to Ninewells Hospital. Ninewells was to become the epicentre for specialised acute services. The transfer of inpatient and outpatient facilities and equipment presented formidable difficulties in adapting a working hospital for such an upheaval.

The most radical change is seen in the A&E Department which is now accommodated in an elephantine extension at the south end of the Concourse Block. It includes a new ambulance entrance and various clinics on the upper floors. A new road cutting through the protected central woodland has been constructed to give a second access from Ninewells Avenue to the A&E Department.

The planning of the new A&E Department sets a new standard, the accommodation having been designed with considerable care. In architectural terms however, the location and form of the extension is very regrettable; it is a medical solution, not an architectural solution. It sits awkwardly in a space configured as a necessary articulation of three major elements, the Main Ward Block, the Concourse Block, and the Minor Ward Block. This space was intended to reveal the dominant south elevation of the Concourse Block, the nodal point in the whole composition (see figure 10). It is now hidden from view and the Hospital Chapel, in its quiet contemplative location, has been removed elsewhere.

The approximate cost of the transfer from DRI is reported as about £26 million. This and other ad-hoc additions on the site have been carried out under PFI contracts.

Fig 28 AW
New extension at south end of the Concourse Block 1998
(sometimes referred to as 'The Casino')

Fig 29 JBE
West Ward Block - 'garden' frontage 2006
Is it acceptable for cars to be parked in front of these windows?

Fig 30 *ALH*
Concourse Block: South Elevation at sundown 1974
N.B. The Hospital Chapel occupied the space at ground level

SITE DEVELOPMENT

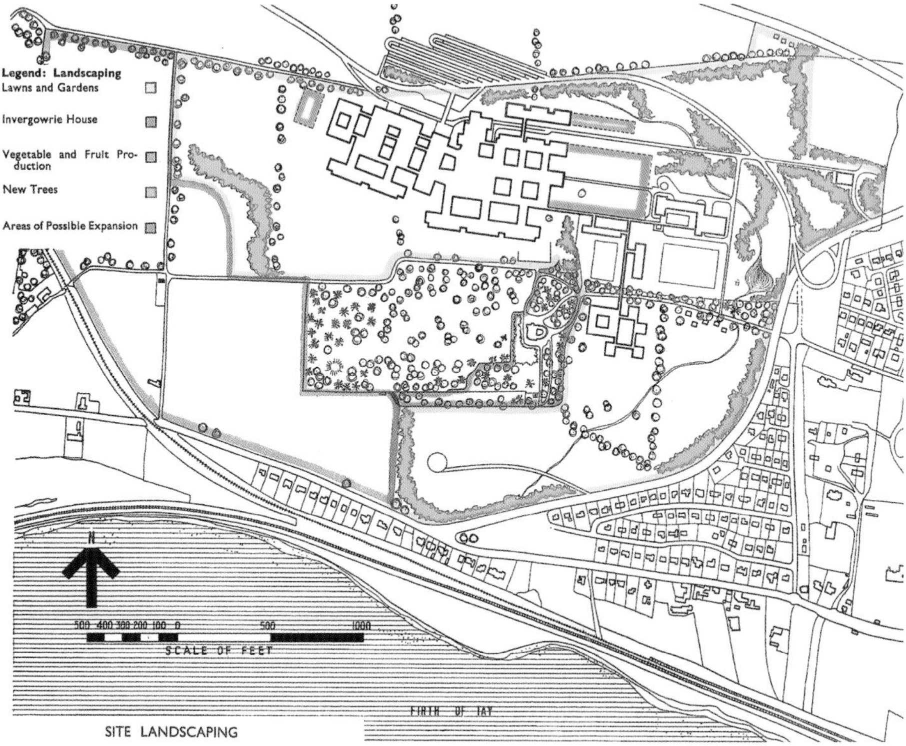

Fig 31 Original concept 1961

The location of the buildings on the site is determined partly by the slope of the ground, (which varies from 10% to 5% southwards), the need to preserve the central woodland, and the presence of the private Invergowrie House situated within the central woodland. The existence of the Lochee sewer which runs diagonally across part of the site is a particular constraint. At a meeting with the City Engineer Mr Armour in January 1960, he explained that :--

a) The sewer dates from 1875, is constructed of brick, and is running to full capacity.

b) It lies fairly close to the surface and thus may interfere with new services ; no building over the line of the sewer is permitted.

c) Re-routing of the sewer would be difficult because of the site contours.

It is said that the development of the site in the past 30 years has been without the benefit of a well considered development plan. In that time one sees an expanded road network (which now connects with new developments west of the Hospital site) and a few unsuitably located car parks. On the western part of the site new buildings have appeared with little coherence in the layout, or assimilation into an overall scheme.

In the belief of the therapeutic value to patients and staff of the external scenery, the intention was for the wards to overlook quiet landscaped gardens and the central woodland of Invergowrie House. All traffic (except fire engines) was to be kept on the north side of the hospital. The Hospital Board provided a substantial budget for a high quality landscape, especially in front of the wards, and for a phased restoration of parts of the central woodland. Many have commented on the disgraceful, unkept appearance of the ground in front of the Main Ward Block, cars parked immediately in front of the windows of the wards in the West Ward Block and rejection of the agreed policy of keeping traffic on the north side of the hospital.

There has been a huge increase in the number of private cars on the site, partly arising from the closure of Dundee Royal Infirmary and an expanding role of the Hospital and Medical School. When cars seeking parking space overflow onto Charleston Drive and Ninewells Avenue, public protest follows. The key question is how can a continuing growth of traffic be contained?

One is reminded of a precept made by Professor Houndsfield, Professor of Engineering at University College London during early debates on construction of motorways, namely that ‘traffic expands to fill the space available’. This observation became part of the lexicon of traffic planning. In the context of Ninewells the word 'space' can be replaced by 'parking space'.

After some lateral thinking, a well known company in Germany who manufacture refrigerators and washing machines and with a workforce of about 2000 were faced with rising numbers of car owners and expanding car parks. The Company gave every employee a free bicycle, negotiated a contract with the local railway company, and turned the car parks into gardens. (Our planning system is devoid of such vision).

The original terraced car park provided spaces for 880 staff cars, with separate entrances and exits to each tier. It is regarded as a successful design which, with more planting, could become relatively unobtrusive. The design allowed for future expansion by completing the upper decks to allow a further 380 parking spaces to give a total of 1260. For unknown reasons this extension has not yet been constructed, but recent ad-hoc addition of car parks at the east end of the site has brought the present total of parking spaces to 2,500.

Fig 32 *AW*
Main Ward Block : 'garden' frontage 2006

Fig 33 *AW*
Approach to Main Entrance 1992

STUMBLING AT THE FIRST HURDLE

Public perception is one of dismay when publicly funded projects fail to be completed on time and within budget. The causes will vary but are often due to a combination of a poorly-drafted Brief, substantially incomplete design prior to issue of tender documents, and late changes. Other factors may be involved, but these are the more significant.
It is self-evident that providing the contractor with necessary information at the critical stages identified in the Programme is a sine qua non for achieving expected progress. An initial period of technical collaboration was intended to determine, by network analysis, the timing for a well-prepared start on site, the critical operations in the programme and the earliest possible date for completion.

The Contractor was appointed in November 1963, but by May 1964 had not produced his Programme. A mitigating factor was the difficulty in obtaining detailed information on medical, hospital and laundry equipment necessary for various key decisions on technical design, especially engineering design. When, in June 1964, the Contractor submitted a claim for loss and expense arising from "enforced delay to a start on site", their misunderstanding of the nature of a parallel working contract was readily apparent.

At a meeting with the firm's Directors in Hawkhill House the question was put to them, "How can you claim for delay when you have not produced the prerequisite for a start on site, namely a Network Programme by which delays can or cannot be verified and measured?" The Directors offered no answer, and appeared not to recognise that, in the absence of such a Programme, the Architect's responsibility for administering the contract was compromised.

When the Contractor claimed that he "was entitled to make a start on site in June and requested the first issue of working drawings", we were in choppy waters. It was in the nature of the contract that working drawings follow, not precede, agreement on the Contractor's programme. The Contractor also claimed that there was no need for a programme in network format and proposed that a conventional bar chart would be satisfactory. For such a complex project, it seemed they were unaware that a bar chart format of a programme was useless.

At this point a moment of epiphany occurred. A Programme Evaluation Group (PEG) was set up under the chairmanship of the Hospital Board's Project Administrator, Robert Paton. It was composed of representatives of the Architect, the Services and Structural Engineers and the Quantity Surveyor. The Group took on the work of programme analysis and the flow of information. The outcome was more satisfactory programming and improved monitoring of progress.

With hindsight, for an innovative project of its size and complexity, an expected six year building programme was unrealistic. It did not take sufficient account that we were in uncharted waters and no allowance in the programme for possible changes had been made.

In more favourable circumstances, with a reasonable adjustment to the programme, the obstacles which were encountered could have been taken in one's stride.

In the event, progressive completion occurred as follows :--

Foundation stone laid	September 1965
Laundry and Boiler House completed	May 1968
Completion of the College of Nursing	May 1969
Completion of the Hospital and Medical School	October 1973
First patients admitted	January 1974

Fig 34 Cutting the First Sod 1964
'Under starters orders': Sir Lewis Robertson and Sir Malcolm Knox

Fig 35 'The Quarry' - an extensive and unforeseeable amount of rock encountered on the northern edge of the site

Fig 36 Construction progress 1967

THE 3-LEGGED STOOL

The administrative responsibilities of the Architect during the building stage comprise the monitoring of quality, cost and time – the 3-legged stool. Speculation arose as to lack of control of costs which were seen to be rising. A distinction needs to be made between the cost of building, cost of equipment (beds, sterilisers, trolleys), expenditure arising from the falling value of money (inflation) and from Government taxes (eg the Selective Employment Tax). The contract contained the usual standard 'rise and fall' clause in respect to labour and materials. There was no 'contract sum' as such, but a Cost Plan which was monitored in cost checks by the Quantity Surveyor as priced schedules of quantity were completed.

The following summary illustrates the make-up of the final building cost :--

Initial cost plan at tender stage	£10,202,000
Additions to the Brief and professional fees	£ 2,334,560
Final measurement including an arbitration award	£ 3,855,000
Total building cost	£16,391,000
Inflation and Selective Employment Tax	£ 3,859,000
Total	£20,250,000

These costs exclude those of the various subsequent ad-hoc additions on site carried out under PFI-type contracts, or otherwise privately funded. The figures are distorted by the fact that certain surgical facilities contained in the Ninewells Brief were 'temporarily' shunted off to Dundee Royal Infirmary for reasons that have not been adequately explained. Taking account of these 'missing' components, the total cost of the Hospital and Medical School was reckoned at about £21.5 million, excluding the cost of the eventual transfer to their rightful home in Ninewells when DRI closed in 1998. The agreed share of the cost between the Hospital Board and the University was 74% and 26% respectively. The reaction of HM Treasury to estimates of the final cost was for a tightening of cost; it became an uneasy struggle to protect the essential provision of 'loose fit'.

With regard to quality, in other European countries major hospitals are generally regarded as a long-term investment of 60 years or more, with specifications based on minimum maintenance costs. Hence the choice for Ninewells of a concrete structure, and precast concrete external cladding with exposed aggregate finish. To ensure that future extensions were to be of similar finish, an assured supply of crushed marble was necessary; this was found at Glanshammer quarry in Sweden; it was delivered by sea direct to Dundee at a lower price than Skye marble (production of which was uncertain). Test panels were made and erected in the mock-up building. The precast panels were made by Scotcon Ltd in Dundee thus enabling ready access for inspections during their production, and also ease of delivery to the site.

Cost planning had to contend with late additions to the Brief for which there was not always a specific budget. In respect to those items comprising the original cost plan, and after allowing for inflation, the over-run in costs was close to the Cost Plan.

As to the time factor, there was no prescribed starting time or completion time in the contract. These times were to be determined in the network programme. It became apparent that the appointed contractor had little or no experience of its use. Without a strategic programme from the Contractor, there would be no formal means by which to guide the production of working drawings.

It has been suggested that hospitals should be designed to a cheaper specification, and to a shorter lifespan. When about 39% of the cost of a modern, well equipped hospital is on engineering services, this suggestion is surely unrealistic.

Fig 37 External cladding showing the ribbon pattern

Fig 38 Erection of test cladding panel 1966 - a critical event

EPILOGUE

The Ninewells solution for a modern teaching hospital is generally seen as an outstanding success, one which in the view of the Scottish Office provided a precedent for future teaching hospitals. The balance between success and possible disappointment is of course the raison d'etre of this study. The key elements of success were :-

Leadership
There was no proliferation of committees with attendant complex and extensive procedures. The Joint Planning Committee, backed by the Joint Technical Committee, acted as the focus of all deliberations.

Joint Working
Recognition by the Hospital Board and the University that preparation of the Brief should go hand in hand with architectural and engineering studies, with selected proposals tested in full-scale mock-ups.

Policy
The concept of the Medical School to be embedded in the Hospital, thus enabling students to be closer to the care of patients, and *"medical research to be carried out under the same roof as real patients"* (Prof Anna Dominizak).

Design
The success of a low rise form of building with provision for adaptability and a means of expansion within an overall architectural concept.

Some failures occurred:-

1. The departure from the policy of a new kind of teaching hospital by the continued use of the obsolete Dundee Royal Infirmary, thus overriding the policy of a unified hospital and medical school on a single site.
2. Failure to ensure that the policy concerning provision for future expansion was understood and implemented.
3. Allowing the contractor to begin substantive work on site without first complying with the necessity to provide a programme in network format.
4. Provision for rotational cleaning and redecoration of the wards by means of a stand-by ward has not been provided.

These events do not diminish the achievement of Ninewells as a modern teaching hospital which is well liked and, as Sir Lewis Robertson found, *"is admired from beyond these shores"*.

It has been suggested that hospitals should be designed to a lower specification and to a shorter lifespan. When about 39% of the cost of a modern hospital is on engineering services, this suggestion is unrealistic. Ninewells is now 35 years old, and with good maintenance and a more efficient heating system it should last for at least a further 35 years (excluding PFI additions).

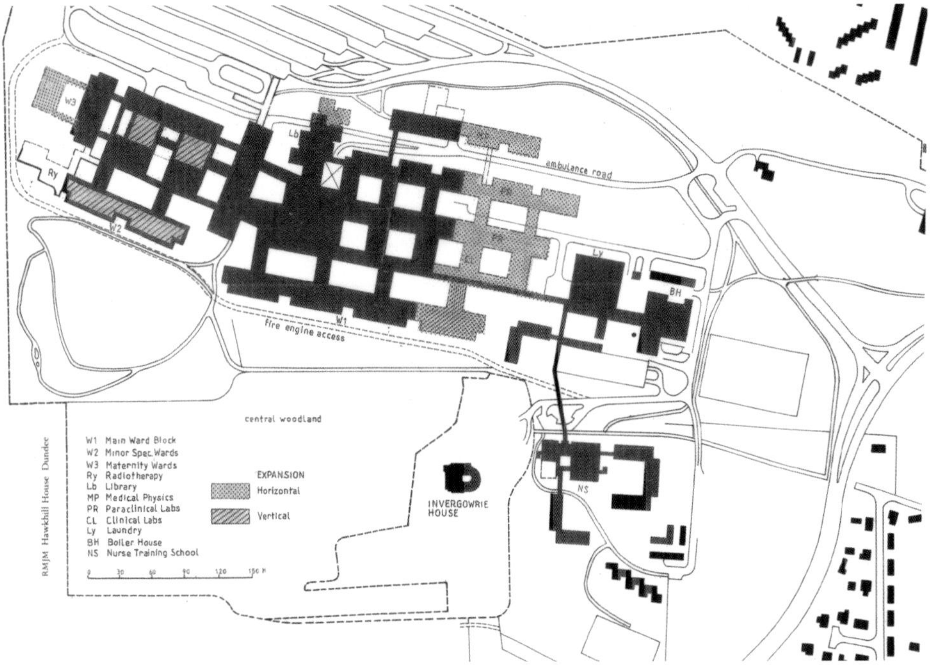

Fig 39 Future Expansion as planned 1964

Fig 40 Ad-hoc growth 1974-2008

Fig 41 The completed hospital looking North West 1974

Fig 42 Ad-hoc growth looking North West 2008

Fig 43 Ninewells Hospital & Medical School. Completion 1974
"For a complex building it has achieved an elegant simplicity" (comment by a visiting delegation of Swedish Architects)

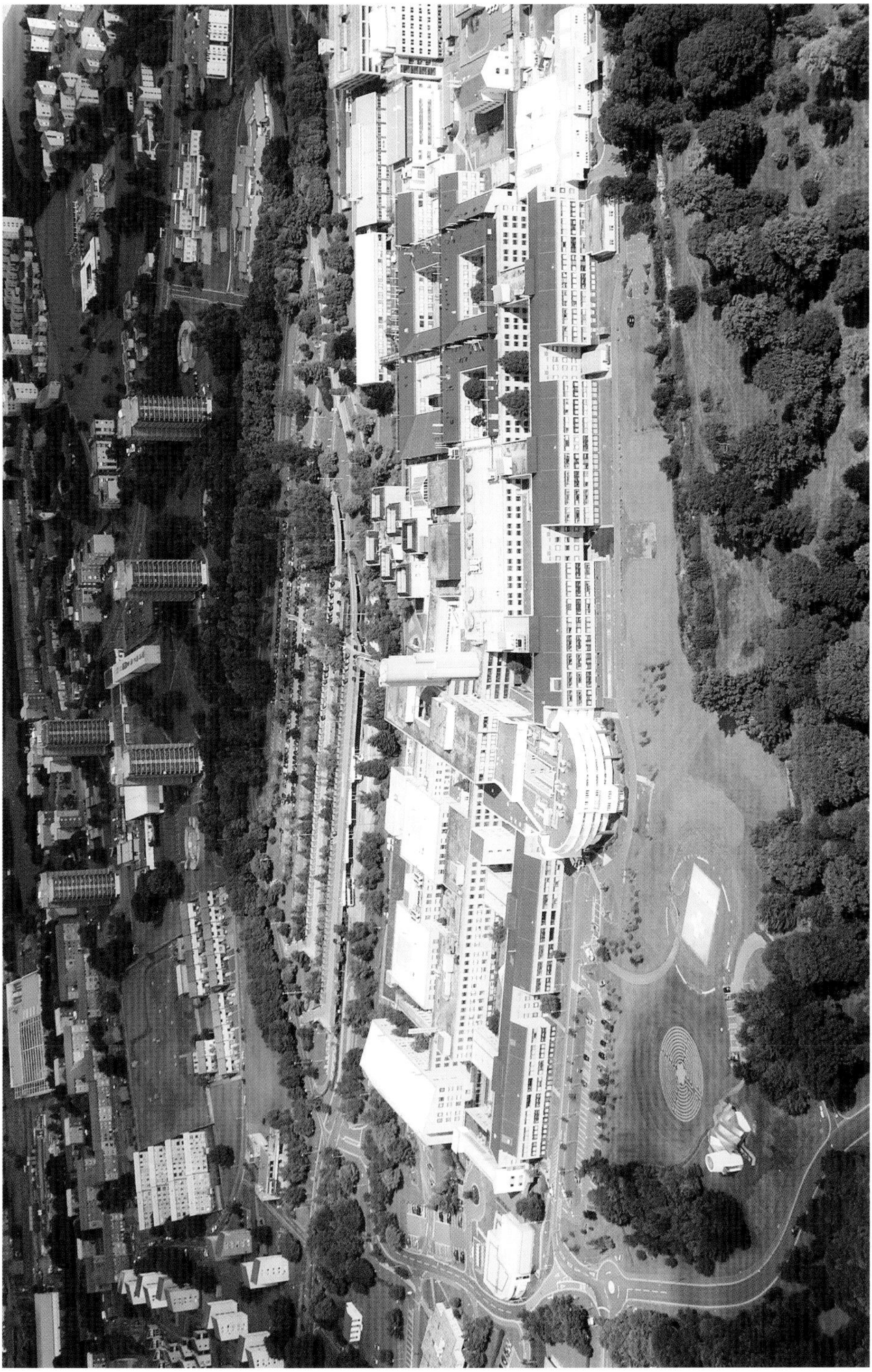

Fig 44 Ninewells Hospital and Medical School Aerial view 2008 - Its wayward growth

POSTSCRIPT

The International Symposium held at Queens College Dundee in 1961 was a landmark in regard to current knowledge at that time of hospital and medical school design. It was particularly beneficial at a critical stage when the drafting of the Ninewells Brief and the design studies were underway.

It is generally recognised that drafting of the Brief in tandem with architectural and engineering studies and with full-scale mock-ups underpinned the success of the Ninewells operation. In particular the programmes of full scale mock-ups engendered confidence that the project had set new standards and that much had been learned about new procedures in medical and nursing practice. As Andrew Hughes of the Department of Health observed, *"A template has been set for future hospital design"*.

At the outset, when the Design Team was being assembled in 1959, a suggestion had been made to establish a joint office on the Ninewells site, thus strengthening links between the Client and within the Design Team in problem solving in programme co-ordination and general progress. Provision of a temporary building could have been regarded as a beneficial investment for the overall good of the project. This proposal unfortunately fell by the wayside.

As to possible misunderstandings regarding the capital cost, Sir Lewis Robertson reaffirmed a general view of Ninewells that *"At about £20 million it was regarded as very good value"*.

APPENDICES

APPENDIX A

KEY EVENTS IN THE BRIEFING, DESIGN AND BUILDING STAGES

Robert Matthew appointed as Architect		1956
Eastern Regional Hospital Board issued outline content of the project		November 1958
Architect's Conceptual Study 'Factors Influencing Height and Bulk'		April 1959
Statement by the Joint Planning Committee of intended Programme		November 1959
Royal College of Surgeons Conference : St Andrews University		May 1960
Architects Journal, Special Issue 'Hospitals : The Big Re-Think'		July 1960
Architects Journal, Editorial re Cardiff Hospital competition		July 1960
Schedules of Accommodation for Hospital & Medical School issued		April 1961
Architect's Scheme Design Report		May 1961
International Symposium, Dundee : 'Hospital and Medical School Design'		July 1961
Architect's Design Reports: --	'Re-appraisal & Prelim Cost Estimate'	December 1961
	'Site Development'	June 1962
	'Engineering Services'	August 1962
Programme of Full-Scale Mock-Ups:	First Stage	June-September 1963
	Second Stage	May-September 1964
	Third Stage	February 1966
Tender documents - Building :	Issued	June 1963
	Received	October 1963
Engineering Services :	Issued	September 1963
	Received	March 1964
Main Contractor appointed		November 1963
Main Engineering Sub-Contractors appointed		April 1964

Contractor start on site	10 August 1964
The HQ of the Design Team, Hawkhill House, Dundee, closed and a new team set up in Edinburgh	April 1965
Final Equipment Schedules issued	August 1965
Foundation Stone laid	9 September 1965
Addition to the Brief of the Radiotherapy Department	April 1966
UGC decision to increase intake of medical students from 60 to 90	June 1966
Queens College Dundee became University of Dundee	May 1967
First patients admitted	January 1974
Official Opening by the Queen Mother	October 1974
Closure of Dundee Royal Infirmary	November 1998

APPENDIX B

Paper presented at the International Symposium, Queens College Dundee 1961 on Hospital and Medical School Design (abridged)

'PLANNING PROCEDURES'

Sir Norman Graham Department of Health for Scotland

Everybody here must be familiar with some hospital planning procedure which takes its colour from the environment and is adapted to circumstances in which it has to operate. I suppose that any one of you who might have been given this assignment would speak primarily to his experience, realising that it might be somewhat peculiar, but hoping to contribute something useful that will help the others. Certainly that is my position.

I intend first to define what, it seems to us in the central Department in Scotland, are the elements of the problem of planning a teaching hospital and the objectives which our procedure should be designed to secure, so far as procedure can. Then I shall describe how we work now, and lastly I shall indicate some of the directions in which we are seeking to improve.

The Elements of the Problem

We are planning quite deliberately for a compromise, because a teaching hospital is a compromise. The fact that most of our best hospitals have had, and have, teaching functions should not obscure the truth - that the treatment of patients and the teaching of medical students are very distinct functions and by no means always compatible. The grouping together under one roof of a series of treatment units that is most convenient for the one purpose is not necessarily the ideal grouping for the other, just as the selection of patients for a particular unit that is based wholly on the urgency of the medical grounds, is not necessarily the best selection for teaching purposes. We are compromising, in another respect. In this country, anyway, our resources - whether one expresses them in financial terms or in real terms as the capacity of the building industry we are going to be severely taxed for as long ahead as we can foresee. We cannot afford to put into a teaching hospital, or any project for which there is a degree of public accountability, more by way of resources than it clearly requires. Running counter to this is a natural tendency for those on the spot to regard the opportunity of building a new hospital as the chance of a lifetime, which indeed, it is, and to want to have everything. The statement of requirements accumulates like a snowball.

Somewhere in the hospital planning exercise the optimum requirements and real resources that can reasonably be deployed have to be brought together, reconciled and matched. This is not simply Treasury control but, in this country, a fact of life.

The third problem is to make a proper appreciation of the functional requirements which the teaching hospital is designed to serve. This seems to be the part of the exercise that is inherently the most difficult and the one that is, even now, the least understood.

Most of us become so accustomed to our working environment that we cease to see how much the physical conditions in which we work and the practices we have inherited influence our pattern of work. Work study has shown that few people know, with any precision of detail, what in fact they do, and how they do it, and I am sure that few of us know all the direct and indirect consequences of our own actions on those of others - the interactions within the working complex, whether it is a hospital or any other sizeable organisation. We have just made a first attempt to analyse the casualty department on these lines and we contemplate a similar study of what actually happens in a series of typical units in a given period who does it; who decides it should be done, and what are the effects of doing it.

At the moment, our planning procedure has to reconcile the need to get on, in spite of the absence of data about the actual operations we are planning to house and provide facilities for. It is not merely a matter of the layout of buildings; this depends on important decisions on working methods and staffing patterns which influence the layout of buildings, and not conversely. The worst decision would be to adopt methods and staffing patterns we have at present. To borrow a phrase from Professor Matthew's First Report on the Ninewells Hospital, the emphasis at this stage is "on function rather than on space".

When Lord Fisher came to the Admiralty in 1904, the British Navy had enjoyed a hundred years' supremacy and had become somewhat complacent - perhaps we have some hospitals like that, and teaching hospitals too. Fisher set up a Committee on Ship Design and laid down at the outset that the strategy ought to determine the ships; the ships must not be allowed to determine the strategy. Some high admirals did not agree, but out of that revolutionary thinking came the all big-gun ship, the Dreadnought, which was revolutionary in its turn and changed the world navies in ten years. Equally, I suggest that throughout our planning we have somehow to keep in view that the patients' needs and the students' needs should determine the design and layout of a teaching hospital (perhaps we may have some high admirals of our own).

The problems cannot be looked at superficially and then thrown, with some attempt at a solution, to an architect, however competent. Long ago a Council of the Eastern Church laid down the essential division of responsibility; "It is for the painters to execute, for the Fathers to order and prescribe". For a teaching hospital in Scotland, the University and the Regional Board are the Fathers and they cannot shuffle out of their responsibility. Here in Dundee, we believe that it has been discharged with a skill and thoroughness that we hope will serve as an example. The measure of success or failure is to be found in the close working arrangements for establishing a Brief and a Design Policy.

The last element of the problem is translation of the careful assessment of functional requirements into a building or series of buildings, an inter-relation of component parts, highly articulated, economically expressed and with some room at likely points for future growth and development. There might have to be compromises at this stage too.

Current Planning Procedure
Now let me turn to the actual procedure we use for hospital planning in Scotland. Those of you from other countries may know that the hospitals here are the Government's responsibility. Virtually the whole expenditure on hospital building is met from public funds. The hospital authorities and we, as a Department, are responsible both for the actual treatment facilities and the teaching facilities that are inseparable from them. The formal teaching facilities are the responsibility of the Universities and the University Grants Committee. There are three objectives:-

1) To ensure that a new building needed by the hospital has been fully assessed and that proposed facilities will fit into a sensible pattern of services.
2 To ensure that the buildings provided are functionally suitable, and
3 To ensure that they are efficient and economical in design and construction

The identification of these objectives is relatively recent. For most of the early years of the National Health Service, so much patching work had to be done that there was no time or occasion to develop general criteria. Now, when we see our way to replace some of the major hospitals we have to work out more closely the basis of our planning.

The regional organisation of hospitals within the National Health Service vests hospital authorities here with an opportunity, not always available elsewhere, to see that there is a precise division of functions as between hospitals in the same area, that the new hospital is in the right place and matches local needs. Whilst it is difficult to establish absolute criteria, we are moving towards a general standard of bed need on which we have been much assisted by independent bodies, such as the Nuffield Provincial Hospitals Trust.

We are collecting comprehensive hospital morbidity statistics for in-patients which should enable us to measure hospital requirements more accurately. We can then work out the functional role of a particular hospital to be built. On outpatient loads and laboratory facilities our data are very imperfect and it will be some time before we can be certain here about the measure of requirements. When we became dismayed at the present system of delegating financial authority to Regional Hospital Boards with the attendant volume of correspondence between the Department and the Boards, we invited hospital authorities to set up for the larger schemes a planning committee in which we could participate directly. It normally consists of representatives of the regional and local Hospital Boards and the University, who clears its own teaching requirements direct with the University Grants Committee.

On the Joint Planning Committee all concerned are at the formative stages of a project and can express their views. The Department can try to influence its shape before it becomes firmly determined by the local people that change becomes a matter for dispute and not agreement. This participation by the Department has been a very instructive discipline. The procedure is a good way of enabling various interests to work together rather than against each other.

The planning committee's main task is to produce a brief for the architect and then to criticise from the client and users point of view, his proposals for the design. It reports at each decisive stage to the principals of the representatives, but to work effectively the Joint Planning Committee needs, and in the Ninewells case has had, a very considerable delegation of authority.

To avoid a series of ad-hoc decisions, the planners must utilise experience other than their own. The first significant hospital planning studies in Britain - on the ward unit- were done by the Nuffield Provincial Hospitals Trust. We started recently in the Department a study of the medium-sized general hospital. The planning teams of several general hospitals to be built in Scotland have examined the constituent elements of each hospital along with our own team for the purpose of sharing experience. One difficulty is keeping the planning up to the pace at which we can build.

There is nothing really exceptional about the application of these procedures in relation to a teaching hospital. In the next decade three of our hospitals in Scotland will be completely rebuilt, three others are to have a major face-lift. There has been no serious difference between the hospital authorities and the medical schools about desirable procedures or overall objectives. Indeed there has been a very high degree of co-operation between the Universities, the Regional Boards, and the Department. The main difficulty has been the scope of the teaching hospital.

It is recognised that it is beyond the capacity of one hospital to house all the facilities needed to teach an annual intake of about 150 students. The days are past in this country when it was almost impossible to conceive of an adequate standard of service except in a teaching hospital. Since the special facilities which a teaching hospital requires make it relatively expensive to construct and to run, we have felt obliged to limit the new hospitals to what seemed an adequate basis for undergraduate and post-graduate clinical teaching and for the research that goes with it, in terms of beds, outpatient facilities and laboratories. Other people have felt that we should try to utilise more fully the exceptional facilities, and the concentration of skills related to a higher proportion of bed capacity.

Against this, we have the fact that people today expect their hospital services to be reasonably near their homes; consequently we should make it easier to travel to and from the hospital, particularly for the growing number of outpatients who have to leave their work, or their homes, to attend for relatively short periods.

It may be that new hospitals on the periphery will draw some potential teaching material away from the teaching hospitals, but on balance we think that any loss can be largely offset by better arrangements for selecting cases for the teaching units. There is also some merit in keeping a hospital to a reasonable size so that it does not become impersonal and does not create such a complexity from the staff's point of view that staff communications become difficult.

Defects in the Procedure

Most of you will have had experience of visiting or, much worse, of working in hospitals that are relatively modern, and yet seeing their striking deficiencies and serious omissions. One wonders who planned these hospitals and how they failed to appreciate what now seem obvious needs.

Are we going to be that wiser? I believe that the most serious weakness in our planning is the lack of collection, collation and digestion of information about requirements we are planning to meet. We start with little reliable and precise data about procedures and activities, there is a mass of established practices, of personal impressions and preferences.

When each of the principals concerned is, if not wayward, at least fallible, and not only mortal, but superannuable, they are not going to take us very far in the useful life of a new hospital. To say this is not to be derogatory to the medical and nursing professions who have had far too few opportunities to respond to the challenge which a new hospital presents.

No procedure can make up for lack of detailed study and analysis of what is happening in other hospitals. Change and progress will often frustrate some of our planning but we are, I suspect, a long way short of getting things as nearly right as it could be. The Assessor for the latest hospital competition in this country wrote in his report that "no radically imaginative or dynamic scheme has emerged from this stimulating challenge to architects". With respect to the Assessor and to his profession, I do not see how any imaginative dynamic scheme can ever emerge without new knowledge and creative thinking .

My second criticism to some extent arises from the first. In the acceptance of real knowledge and a doctrine firmly based on knowledge, planning a hospital is a subject on which everyone thinks, with some justice, he can pronounce with as much authority as anyone else. Thus everyone expects to be consulted; and planning committees become too big to placate all the interests that demand representation; sub-committees then proliferate. It is magnificently democratic but it is not planning. Even where the people on the committees take a huge amount of time and trouble in an effort to contribute from their own experience, the experiences are too varied, and have never been analysed and compared, so the exercise tends to become incoherent, inordinately time-consuming and frustrating for everybody. The maximum consultation seems merely to produce the minimum result. We cannot go on in this fashion.

This brings me to my third point. Our procedure so far does not produce results quickly enough. We all become so fascinated with the problems of space that we seem to forget about time. In Scotland we are especially conscious at this moment of the time factor because, after many vicissitudes, we face a prospect of much re-building of the major teaching hospitals that is sadly overdue. These projects take time to mature, but it is hard, even for a slow moving bureaucracy, to be content with slow progress. It is so much easier to discuss than to come to a decision. While one ought to be able to discuss without becoming offensive, it is seldom that one can decide without offending somebody. I hope that, in planning these large hospitals, we now have the experience to know what a realistic time schedule should be and the conviction to make people observe it.

Finally, I want to mention two gaps in procedure which must be filled. Assumptions as to how the work should be carried out are based either on the advice of individuals or and I hope progressively more so - on detailed study and analysis. We should then be able to produce a design which is reasonably well suited to the functions the building is intended to serve.

At this point the first gap occurs. Our procedure does nothing to ensure that those who will work in the new hospital, or even their leaders, will understand the design assumptions and readily put them into practice to full effect. As a colleague of mine observed: "Polynesians would no doubt be able to take a modern destroyer across the Pacific, but they would take it under sail". Unless we close the gap in our procedures, the new hospitals now on the drawing board will, when they come into commission, be more subject to the winds and tides of personal preference than they should be. The full power of their engines, so to speak, will not be utilised because no-one will have been taught how to operate them. Just as no airline would bring in a new type of aircraft without sending their most experienced pilots and their maintenance engineers on a conversion course, so we require a very thorough and comprehensive effort to ensure that all who will occupy a position of responsibility in a new hospital know when they gets there what it contains, why it is there, and how it is used. If we are to improve we shall need criticism from knowledge and not from ignorance.

The second gap is the lack of a systematic review of what we do build. Until we have more experience we ought, at some stage, to examine the efficiency of each new unit in practice, to assess it, and to identify the real causes of its shortcomings.- they will not always be the apparent causes. We should then acknowledge and publicise them, so that they are not repeated. We had better recognise, from the start, that we shall make mistakes, if for no other reason than we do not yet know enough about the problems which we are seeking to solve.

APPENDIX C

MEMORANDUM : **Factors Influencing the Height and Bulk of the Buildings for the Hospital and Medical School** *Alan Wightman*

Scale

a) Habitable Environment

The apprehension of the patient or child coming into a strange environment could be allayed to some degree if the change from the familiar to the new is lessened as much as possible. A domestic scale (say 1-3 storeys) of the ward blocks could make a considerable contribution in this respect.

b) Working Environment

Most of us are accustomed to an increase in scale of the working environment (offices, shops, etc) and therefore an increase in the height and size of the working parts of the Hospital and Medical School (laboratories, theatres etc) is to be expected. Even so there must be some limit beyond which an increase in the height and bulk within a very large complex could be overpowering.

Identity

A sense of "where one is" and "where one belongs" in such a diverse building can give the patient, visitor, and member of staff a sense of immediate loyalty to his or her unit, factors which can interact on one another. This applies to the wards in particular where identity and a degree of separate expression is desirable.

Enclosure and Proportion

For functional reasons (see later) the various units of a Hospital & Medical School could be related rather loosely. The size of open spaces created in such an arrangement of units of buildings will influence the height of the buildings enclosing such units. This is mainly a matter of visual proportions, namely height to spacing. Other factors are involved in these judgements such as daylight and sunlight penetration.

External Views

In all weathers the close view, as compared with the long view, for the bed-ridden patient can usually give more interest and stimulation. For example being able to see the colour and developing forms of growing plants, and the changing texture of trees. Is this not why visitors bring flowers to the wards? Assuming the therapeutic value of such views to the patient, and also the nurse, nearness to the ground is beneficial.

Adaptability

Ease of extension and adaptability are primary factors influencing the form of a building. The probable order of importance for achieving an appropriate degree of adaptability is :--

Research and diagnostic laboratories
The Wards
The Polyclinic

Adaptable planning needs a degree of detachment, consistent with clean and tight planning, between various elements which can most easily be achieved by a low rise development - it is easier to grow sideways than upwards.

Planning & Form

a) Circulation

The greater the degree of concentration of circulation spaces, the more will be savings in construction and in maintenance costs. Clarity of organisation and plan with simple direct routes is a prerequisite; this should be achievable with either a vertical or a horizontal form of development.

b) Travelling Time

Studies in America by Isadore and Zachary Rosenfield (hospital consultants) have shown that vertical travel usually takes 3 to 4 times as long compared with the equivalent horizontal travel. This is due to time spent in waiting and riding in relatively slow hospital lifts. Also they showed that the complex traffic loads which occur in clinical and diagnostic departments can be better organised if these departments are located as close together as possible on one or two floors. This means not only a saving in time for staff, but also greater ease of interdepartmental consultations. Anthony Jennings has quoted studies in four African hospitals, (1500 beds,700 beds,300 beds, and 220 beds) in which departmental journeys were measured over a period of 18 months. These studies showed that clinical relationships between departments are better satisfied by a horizontal rather than a vertical development.

Effort and Pedestrian Movement

Dr Maumy has referred to studies in Paris on the energy expended in walking upstairs and on the level. It was calculated that the effort in mounting one stair is equivalent to covering a flat distance L itself equal to 5 times the height H of the stair, thus L=5H. Mechanised means of pedestrian movement obviously produce a different comparison, but no studies have apparently been made. In regard to lifts, whilst no effort is used in travelling vertically, the waiting time can be a source of considerable irritation which leads to mental fatigue. This waiting time is a frequent source of complaint in many American high-rise buildings. Is this not why some people find waiting for lifts, or buses, more tiring than walking a limited distance? Where the density of traffic justifies, the escalator for pedestrian movement up to three or four floors has clear advantages over the lift. A single escalator has a capacity of about 9,000 persons per hour when used horizontally as a moving pavement. The engineer, Felix Samuely, has supported greater use of moving pavements in heavy trafficked areas such as railway stations. Escalators might have a useful role in large hospitals of say two or three storeys where the main traffic generating spaces can be concentrated, such as the arrival concourse. Issuing scooters to staff, as in the Karolinska Hospital in Stockholm, may be an appropriate solution for long corridors; but how long is "long"?

The Ground Floor

The ground floor is the most valuable level of circulation for reasons of access to the building for people and goods. The greater the choice in locating points of access to a building, the more flexible will be the circulation system to meet future changes. The sloping site at Ninewells is a big advantage because it offers the possibility of segregation of internal traffic.

Structure
Other factors being equal, a tall building will usually cost more than the equivalent accommodation in a low building. There is no complete explanation as to why this should be so. A tall structure has to meet very strict standards of fire safety, and withstand high wind loads. A low structure will have a larger footprint which might increase the cost of piped services and foundations.

Fire Precautions
The predominant fire risk to human life in a hospital is the sleeping population in the wards who will need help to escape from a fire. Evacuation of the building thus presents potential difficulties. To extend the time for escape, fire-safety compartments can be provided so enabling two-stage evacuation of a building. In a tall building the second stage of evacuation i.e. of all patients and staff from the building, could be difficult, partly because the "flue effect" in tall buildings is a major hazard. There is also the risk of failure of the electrical installation putting the lifts out of use. Hence the importance of being able to escape to an adjacent fire-safety compartment on the same level.

The predominant fire risk in the laboratories, operating theatres, pharmacy etc arises from the quantity of inflammable material and explosive risks which are present. This calls for the isolation of particular risks by the provision of fire compartments. Certain special fire risks arising for example with inflammable liquid stores, paint spraying, nitrate stores, will need to be isolated in separate buildings which are readily accessible by the Fire Brigade.

Space Heating
There appears to be no decisive factor influencing the choice of the heating system for a low or high rise development. Much depends on compactness of the scheme, ready accessibility of services, and choice of the distribution medium, water or air.

Ventilation
The traditional Nightingale ward depended on natural ventilation. This worked well with high ceilings and cross ventilation over the width of the ward whereby air currents can be readily induced. The ward sister's quick "blow through" each morning was standard practice.

To achieve a reasonable degree of compactness in a low-rise development, deep planning is likely to feature. It calls for mechanical ventilation with very low noise levels. Whether in a low-rise or high-rise scheme, if ward planning is based to a significant degree of single rooms, then mechanical ventilation might need to be extended to air-conditioning.

Lighting
Penetration of daylight and sunlight is influenced by the aspect of a building, by the nearness of other buildings, and by design of windows. In the centre of a low-rise deep planned layout it is vital to ensure a minimum degree of daylight, and for occasional external views. Small courtyards in carefully chosen locations can help to relieve claustrophobia, and feelings of disorientation.

Noise Transmission
A tall compact building usually creates the most difficulties in respect to the transmission of airborne sound, especially via lift shafts and stairwells. Structure-borne sound can, at a cost, be reduced by suitable detailing of the construction. In tall buildings fire lobbies may help to lessen noise transmission.

Passenger Lifts
In studies by Isadore and Zachary Rosenfield in the USA of proposals for new 1000 bed hospitals for Palo Alto and Stanford University, they compared two ideas, one for an 18-storey tower block with a 2-storey spread out base, the other a low-rise scheme of two/three storeys. They found that the tower scheme would need at least 10 lifts whereas the low rise scheme required only 4 lifts, giving at the same time a much better service. Also in the tower, the lifts consumed 18,000 sq.ft of floor space compared with 1,600 sq.ft for the low rise scheme. Estimated savings in costs for the low rise scheme as compared to a high rise scheme were found to be $865,000 on lift installation, $300,000 on the structure. In addition to capital costs, maintenance and insurance costs, lifts are a substantial item in the budget.

[In a building erected in 2005 in Scotland the quoted sum for the maintenance of five lifts is £785 per annum, (excluding cost of spare parts). The initial cost of an escalator serving one floor is about £17,000 per pair (one up one down).The capacity of an elevator is equivalent to about 3 lifts costing about £35,000. For the same situation of 3 floors an escalator would cost about £50,000. Such a cost could only be justified where a dense concentration of traffic exists.]

Mechanical Conveyors
There appears to have been no systematic study of the economics of horizontal as compared with vertical conveyors (dumb waiters). It would appear to be easier to convey articles, such as food trays, vertically rather than horizontally, but much will depend on the extent to which accommodation can be grouped along a simple direct route between source and destination. Such direct routes are easier to plan in a tower rather than a low rise scheme.

In the United Mineworkers Hospitals in the USA a system of horizontal & vertical conveyors known as "trayveyors", was used to convey made-up meals on trays to the wards; on return they be automatically loaded into a dishwashing machine. This type of facility is suitable for a compact hospital in a high wage economy.

Pneumatic Tubes
Many hospitals are now using pneumatic tubes for conveying items such as prescription drugs, X-ray films etc. They save labour, save time and offer security. There appears to be no deciding factor in respect of cost for a horizontal against a vertical scheme. Indeed a characteristic of pneumatic tube installation is that it is suited to a mixed development of low and high density. A comparatively loose spread out development presents no appreciable disadvantage. Other things being equal, the more compact the layout the more economical the installation.

Plumbing
The greatest economies in water supplies and drainage will usually be achieved when pipes are grouped in vertical ducts and where there is a high standard of repetition such as in the wards. This may not be possible in extensive laboratory accommodation where the need for a horizontal grouping applies, and a degree of flexibility is essential. For low rise buildings the high cost of mains distribution of services calls for minimum frontages in all types of accommodation, but especially laboratories.

Wards
Certain ward units at Ninewells are required to be physically separate from other wards for reasons of cross infection. This includes the maternity and paediatric wards. Such a requirement appears to indicate a minimum of four groups of wards. The wards serving each Specialty need to be as close as possible to their respective clinical departments. This is best achieved in a horizontal relationship. The largest group of wards are those of medicine and surgery each comprising six wards.

Some built-in teaching and administrative facilities at Ninewells might be shared between adjacent wards if they are on the same level. This suggests two wards per floor as a minimum. From current studies, the floor area of a typical ward unit might be as much as 12,000 sq feet. If placed in a tall building it would result in a form of considerable bulk. In the event of an epidemic of a contagious disease, barrier nursing is more likely to be achieved where the wards were grouped in a suitable horizontal arrangement, as against being located in a vertical stack.

Site Characteristics
The extent of the site at Ninewells, and more particularly those portions of it most favourable for building, is sufficient not to exercise any decisive limits on the form of development. From our present knowledge of the site there appears to be no particular influence on the form of the hospital from the likely means of access. It was agreed with the City Engineer to restrict the number of vehicle entrances to no more than two. As previously noted, with a low rise building, the sloping site provides the opportunity of access at different levels and hence a separation of different types of traffic.

Locating the hospital complex on the north side of the central woodland of Invergowrie House would offer some shelter against the prevailing wind and possibly offer some reduction in noise from traffic on the Perth Road.

Building Operations
To minimise building costs and enable the hospital to be erected in the shortest possible time, a choice of the building form needs careful study in respect of the contractor's operations. The height and bulk of the building will influence the way in which the Contractor decides to plan his operations, especially the use of cranes. It is not possible at this distance in time to forecast how a contractor would plan his operations except to say that a low-rise scheme may offer advantages of two or three teams in different sections of the building, if not simultaneously, then with a degree of overlap.

Summary

The aim of designing the project on predominantly two or three storeys is recommended for the following reasons :-

Scale	The feeling of closeness to the ground , awareness of the outside world and the changing landscape.
Compactness -	Planning in depth by means of internal courtyards for light and air and avoidance of claustrophobia.
Adaptability -	Open ended planning where growth can be anticipated, for example in the paraclinical departments.
Circulation -	Ease of movement throughout the Hospital and Medical School between closely related activities.
Access -	Location of entrances to take advantage of the sloping site and thus enable a degree of traffic segregation.
Safety -	Ease of escape in case of fire from the wards, treatment areas, laboratories and other relatively “confined” spaces.
Simplicity -	Standardisation of space planning and building methods in the interest of cost, adaptability, and ease of maintenance.

The adoption of a low-rise scheme need not imply sprawl. The principle of what one can call “courtyard planning” enables an acceptable degree of deep planning to be achieved and a significant provision for future horizontal expansion. The outcome might be described as a loose knitting together of the various parts in a way that meets the needs of compactness, adaptability, and a satisfactory scale of development.

Alan Wightman RMJM April 1959

APPENDIX D

BUILDING DESIGN & HOSPITAL ACQUIRED INFECTION

In the fight against hospital acquired infection (HAI), building design has been generally regarded as less important than hospital staff, visitors to the hospital, patients, medical and ancillary staff, cleaners, plumbers, etc. The question, much discussed in the early design stages, was how can building design contribute to lowering the incidence of HAI ?

In a lecture to architects in 1963 Professor Williams, Professor of Bacteriology at the University of London, stated *"current research by bacteriologists has demonstrated the enormous extent to which pathogenic bacteria can be carried around a hospital on air currents. We must therefore endeavour to avoid transfer from one area of the hospital to another"*.

At the time Professor Williams' views were widely accepted and provided a basis for certain design principles, for example:-

a) Zoning: The physical separation of clean and dirty environments
b) Airlocks: To control ingress of air currents into a clean zone
c) Dilution: Ensuring a steady flow of tempered air in the wards in order to avoid a build up of potentially contaminated air

These principles were applied in four important areas:-

1) Operating theatres: The traditional twin theatres were ruled out. All theatres were to be self-contained with separation of clean arrival traffic from dirty disposal traffic. This also meant no shared ventilation or preparation space.
2) Treatment rooms to be provided on the wards with a good standard of aseptic control, and protected by airlocks.
3) Maintaining the open bays of a typical ward in the interests of ensuring the designed rate of air-flow.
4) Teaching rounds in the wards to cease, and be replaced by student teaching in a Demonstration Room and Tutorial Room on each Ward Unit.

In later years new knowledge has indicated other ways by which building design can help, for example fitting of sensors to doors and tap handles to avoid hand contact. Research in Scandinavia had revealed that one of the biggest reservoirs of pathogens is in the floor covering; hence carpets were ruled out in clinical areas.

The view that HAI would be lessened significantly by the provision of a greater number of single rooms on the wards is sometimes heard; in discussions on ward planning it was found that there was no good evidence to support such a view. It is now recognised that observance of personal hygiene is much more significant. It is a matter of concern that Treatment Rooms on the wards are now much less used, some not at all.

APPENDIX E

ISAMBARD KINGDOM BRUNEL

Few will be unaware of this extraordinary man, structural engineer, mechanical engineer, architect, and ship designer. It may be asked what is the relevance of Brunel to a study of hospital design? The answer lies in the disaster of the Crimean War (1854-56) where the deaths of the sick and wounded soldiers exceeded deaths in battle.

When Florence Nightingale, following a visit to the Crimea, remonstrated with Government ministers about serious deficiencies of the medical services and the unsanitary and overcrowded conditions of the 'hospitals' there, a political storm arose. Her campaign to force the Government to take action resulted in the appointment of Brunel. He was given authority to do whatever was necessary for the design of *"a hospital system capable of rapid erection, and of providing a safe environment for patients, nurses, and medical staff"*. That was his Brief. Brunel began work immediately on the design of a prefabricated timber system of construction, using a high degree of repetition in the component parts. In six days he had placed the contract for the supply of materials and components, including sanitary and ventilation equipment, for a hospital of 1000 beds.

In explaining his design principles, Brunel stated *"the aggregate of the building should consist of such parts as can be conveniently united to make one whole under great variations of conditions in the form and nature of the site, and that the building must be capable of extension by the consistent addition of the parts"*.

The principle of 'extendibility' was fundamental to Brunel's approach, as were environmental requirements in respect of hygiene, comfort, and cleanliness. A full scale prototype of a typical ward was erected in Paddington Station London.

The planned 22 wards were in the form of standard pavilions attached to a spine corridor along which it was intended to run a railway bringing the sick and wounded from the boats arriving from the war zone at Sebastopol. The first consignment of building parts were landed in May 1855 and by December the three pavilions of the Hospital, consisting of 6 wards, had been completed.

Brunel's concern for good ventilation and sanitation included a manually operated forced ventilation system calculated to supply 1000-1500 cu feet of air per minute to each patient. All wards were supplied with a piped water supply, flushing toilets and a *"perfect system of drainage from every building to a safe distance from the hospital"*.

In spite of the severest forms of disease a death rate of 0.3% at Renkoi compares with a death rate of 42% at the previous 'hospital' at Scutari.

It can be said that Brunel's genius lay in his ability to identify the principles on which solutions are to be based for the planning of a hospital, and for building and environmental design which take account of the indeterminate nature of the project. The fact that Brunel also gave equal attention to the logistical factors inherent in the organisation of the project underlines the genius of the man.

To quote David Toppin's description of achievement at the Renkoi hospital:-
"The correctness of Brunel's perceptive grasp of human needs, and failings, and his understanding of the measures necessary to deal with both, in addition the fundamental importance of organisation and environmental standards, showed a man of prodigious powers".

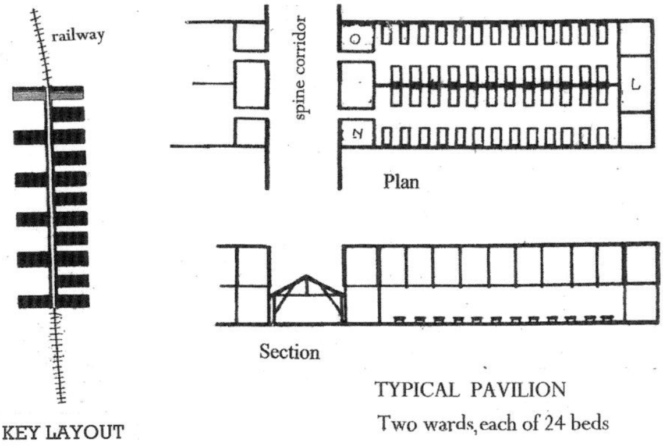

We gratefully acknowledge the permission of Arup Scotland to use extracts from David Toppin's monograph of Brunel and his hospital at Renkoi. David Toppin trained as a civil engineer at Manchester prior to studying and becoming a tutor at the Architectural Association School of Architecture, London.

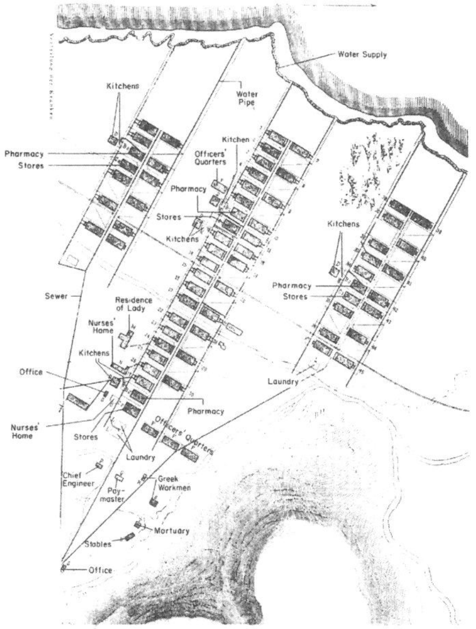

Fig 45: Plan of I. K. Brunel's extendible hospital at Renkioi 1855

APPENDIX F REFERENCES

July 1960	The Architects Journal 'The Hospital Brief'
May 1961	Robert Matthew & Johnson-Marshall : Design Report and Preliminary Sketch Plans
June 1961	International Symposium, Queens College, Dundee 'Hospital and Medical School Design' Editor, George Bell
December 1961	The Lancet 'From Words to Wards' Dr T. Sommerville and A.Wightman
March 1962	Musgrave Park Hospital, Belfast The Nuffield Foundation
July 1962	The Lancet 'Operating Theatre Design' Professor Donald Douglas
January 1964	Symposium, The Royal College of Surgeons, London. 'Operating Theatres & Ancillary Rooms'
June 1965	The Architectural Review 'Health and Hospitals'
July 1966	Journal of the Royal College of Surgeons of Edinburgh 'The Prevention of Hospital Infection by Design' R.R.Gillies 'Theatre Suite Design in relation to Hospital Infection' Professor Donald Douglas
1966	Moderna Sjukhus (Modern Hospital, International Issue) Editor : Sven Kahn
January 1967	Royal Scottish Society of Arts; The Keith Lecture 'Trends in Operating Theatre Design' Sir Robert Matthew
1982	'University Education in Dundee 1881-1981' Michael Shafe
1986	'British Hospitals and Health-Care Buildings' Architectural Press Edited by Peter Stone
1987	'The History of Medicine in the University of St Andrews' John S G Blair
1998	'Dundee Royal Infirmary 1798-1998' Norman Watson
2008	'Modern Architect, The Life and Times of Robert Matthew' Miles Glendinning

APPENDIX G QUOTATIONS

"There is much to learn from the experience of the Ninewells project. Before the collective memory fades, I believe a record of lessons learned, both in terms of procedures and of design, should be compiled. As one who was in close touch with the architect team it was evident that an insight into the Client/Architect relationship in the work of preparing the Brief and assessing the Design options is so important".
Dr Tom Sommerville, Department of Bacteriology, Queens College, Dundee
International Symposium on Hospital and Medical School Design, Dundee 1961

"There is a need for systematic post-audit appraisals of architectural and of engineering design during the first decade of the life of the building. These would make an invaluable contribution to the advancement of our knowledge of hospital and medical school design".
Dr Jack Masur, Asst Surgeon General and Director of the Clinical Centre of National Institutes of Health, Bethesda, Maryland USA
International Symposium Queens College, Dundee 1961.

"Our procedure does nothing to ensure that those who will work in the new hospital, or even the leaders, will understand the design assumptions and readily put them into practice to full effect. What is required is a very thorough effort to ensure that everyone who will occupy a position of responsibility in a new hospital knows when he gets there, what it contains, why it is there, and how it is to be used".
Sir Norman Graham, Department of Health for Scotland
International Symposium Queens College, Dundee 1961

"The policy of embedding the Medical School enables the teaching function to reach beyond the systematic lecture to the tutorial method of learning close to the patient But let us be aware, the most important single factor causing outbreaks of hospital infection is OVERCROWDING. In preventative medicine, and hospital architecture is now a branch of preventative medicine, attention to detail is all-important".
Dr Tom Sommerville, Dept of Bacteriology, Queens College, Dundee
The Architects' Journal, July 1960

"In the interests of both efficiency and economy, we have to recognise that the need, and the implications, for centralisation of certain routine functions may, and perhaps should, extend beyond the single hospital to an appropriate group of hospitals".
J K Johnston, Secretary to the Eastern Regional Hospital Board
Architects Journal, July 1960

"The difficulties encountered with this pioneering scheme were considerable and though some mistakes were made, they were largely due to inexperience and not misdemeanour".
Sir Malcolm Knox, Principal of the University of St Andrews
International Symposium Queens College, Dundee 1961

"Make no mistake about it, whatever hitches there may have been, this is going to be one of the outstanding hospital and medical teaching project of the generation unique in Scotland, practically unique in the United Kingdom and a matter for proper pride in the Dundee area, and in Scotland as a whole".
Sir Lewis Robertson, Chairman of the Eastern Regional Hospital Board,
Press Conference Dundee 25 April 1969

"A universal defect in hospital planning today is the failure to appreciate the rate of change, and the continuously rising demand for both routine and research laboratories. What is research today becomes routine tomorrow".
Dr Jack Masur,
International Symposium, Queens College, Dundee, 1961

"It is important that building committees acknowledge the real speciality of the architect which is to gather together all considerations, to weigh all conflicting interests, and out of this to form a whole which is right, and looks right. This is the task of the architect, for architecture is a language, not just a decoration".
Preben Hansen MAA, Architect, Copenhagen

"Carrying out research under the same roof as patients is an important step towards translating medical discoveries into effective treatments faster and better".
Professor Anna Dominiczak
Director of the Cardiovascular Research Centre, Glasgow

"In a project of this complexity it is difficult to over-emphasise the value of a small planning team on which the Architect and the Consultant Services Engineer are represented, working full time on the problems involved. The early establishment of such a team enabled detailed studies to proceed in tandem with those on functional requirements, mechanical services and architectural design".
Sir Robert Matthew,
International Symposium, Queens College, Dundee, 1961

"When a future extension is needed for Ninewells it will pose some difficult architectural problems if the quality and cohesion of the scheme, as presently built, is to be maintained. The fear is not so much of an ad-hoc response to a minor problem, the solution to which is straightforward; this is part of the process of growth and change. The fear is that, when the time comes to make a major addition to Ninewells, the necessary architectural standard which preserves the unity of the scheme will not be achieved. If that were allowed to happen it would be a disaster".
Peter Stone, Architect

"A large teaching hospital developed over ten years on a modest scale, generally with three storey height. New facilities include teaching blocks with wards next to clinical teaching, and clinical research, next to basic sciences. A well thought out solution elegantly executed".
Architects Journal August 1982

APPENDIX H

TEMPLATE FOR A FUTURE SIMILAR PROJECT

It has been suggested that the Ninewells project provides a template for similar projects in respect of the formulation of the Brief and the Design as a seamless process. For a similar project the objective should be the adoption of a unified process of drafting the Brief, the Design principles, and the Programme in which quality, cost and time are seen as a '3-legged stool'.

The following is little more than an outline of an appropriate strategy:--

1) Adopt a structure for the Client body similar to the Ninewells model in order to ensure a balance between necessary consultations, and action.

2) Form a progress evaluation group (PEG) consisting of a member of the Client, the Architect, the Engineer and the Quantity Surveyor in order to spearhead progress at all stages by reference to a Network Programme.

3) Provide the shortest possible lines of communication, with the Design Team under one roof, located close to the Client representatives.

4) In the initial stage, allocate time for preliminary studies to test ideas and propositions in tandem with the drafting of the Brief.

5) To assist understanding of the architectural studies/proposals, models are an important tool in the design process, supplemented where necessary by selected items for a full-scale mock-up.

6) Tenders for the building work and engineering services to be received on the same date to enable assessments to be made on both cost and programme.

7) In a parallel working type of contract, the building contract should define appropriate procedures, including the stages for formal Cost Reports by the Quantity Surveyor and Interim Certificates/Reports by the Architect.

8) Where items of significant uncertainty arise in the drafting of the specification a contingency sum should be allotted to each particular item.

9) Schedules of client equipment and other items, the selection of which is the responsibility of the Client, to be identified, if possible in the Brief, otherwise at times determined by the Network Programme.

10) Selection of specialist firms, whose design skills, specialist technical skills or experience are needed to be identified in the Specification.

11) Contractors invited to tender are required to provide an outline of their approach to the planning and organisation of the contract.

12) A Commissioning Manual to be prepared for the Client explaining design and operational policies upon which the project is based. These to include functional design, measure of adaptability, and provision for expansion.

13) As a supplement to the Manual, a Maintenance Guide to be prepared which identifies, for example, time to first maintenance, expiry times of any guarantees, expected lifespan of components etc.

14) If there is to be a phased hand-over, the legal implications and practical arrangements to be set out in the contract documents.

ADDENDUM

A supplement to this study, 'Ninewells Revisited', covering a difficult and troublesome period following the disbandment of the Hawkhill House team could only be written if all relevant records of the Eastern Regional Hospital Board, the University and the Scottish Office were to become available.

March 2009

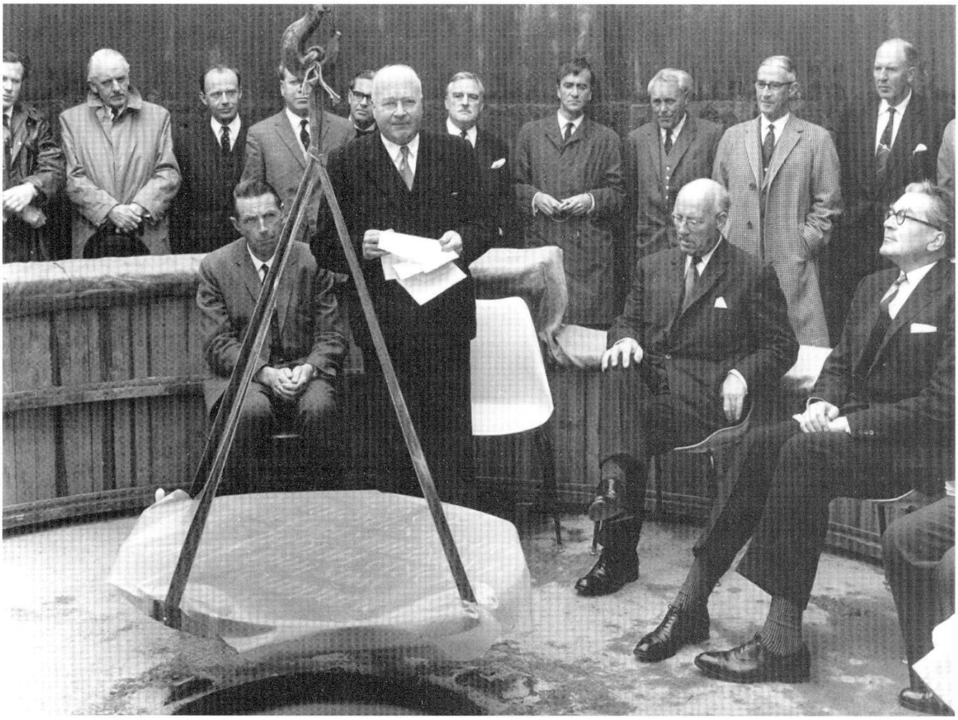

The Ailsa Craig stone was designed by the distinguished sculptor Maxwell Allan

Fig 46 and 47 The Foundation Stone Ceremony 1965

Sir Malcolm Knox (centre above), Sir Lewis Robertson (far right above), Lord Hughes of Hawkhill (with gavel)

Sir Lewis Robertson

Sir Malcolm Knox

Professor Robert Hunter

Professor Donald Douglas

Dr Tom Sommerville

Dr James Hunter

JK Johnston

Sir Robert Matthew

Fig 48 Key Players